Step-By-Step:
Deception in Defence

Barry Rigal

B. T. Batsford Ltd, *London*

First published 1997

© Barry Rigal

ISBN 0 7134 7841 1

A CIP catalogue record for this book is available from the British Library.

Typeset by Apsbridge Services Ltd, Nottingham.
Printed by Redwood Books, Trowbridge, Wiltshire
for the publishers,
B. T. Batsford Ltd, 583 Fulham Road,
London SW6 5BY

A BATSFORD BRIDGE BOOK
Series Editor: Tony Sowter

CONTENTS

INTRODUCTION

People get their pleasures from bridge in vastly different ways. Some people see the bidding as merely being the prelude to the serious business of the play of the cards – and it is certainly true that there is little point in threading your way through the Scylla of 3NT and the Charybdis of four spades to a delicate contract of five clubs if you are going to go down by failing to count trumps.

Some people get their pleasure by simply playing well, that is to say by not making mistakes. There are players I know who firmly believe that if they can accomplish the difficult task of not making errors, that is the highest level of the game; if they lose, at least it will be someone else's fault. I find this view a little impractical – even ignoring the fact that very few can aspire to playing error-free bridge. Having said that, it is arguable that you can succeed at every level of bridge by simply making the par bid and the par play. If you bid every game that should be bid, and succeed in every makeable contract you will be a fearsome opponent. But deception is not like that: the object of a deceptive play is to help to defeat the lay-down contract, and to succeed in the impossible one. In other words you are seeking to beat par – and in my opinion the successful deceptive play is the one that yields the most pleasure, because in achieving your aim you have thwarted fate; the fact that you may have embarrassed your friend or opponent at the same time may add to your pleasure – it certainly does to mine. I am not above admitting to enjoying the experience of *Schadenfreude*.

If that is the case for you too, then you may also feel, as I do, that deception in defence is in many ways the richest, most complex, dangerous, and ultimately satisfying area of the game. It is certainly arguable that deception in defence is more fun than declarer deception. The reason that it is more dangerous for a defender to try to deceive than it is for declarer is because of the existence of your partner. Some people view defence as one player issuing instructions and the other player obeying the command (that is after all what a 'come-on' signal equates to). On the other hand a lot of good defence involves situations where one defender can not take control, because he may not know what to do; instead he signals to his partner to let him take that decision based on full information. That is why deceptive defence can cause problems; when you feed a false message to partner you are usurping control from him, and playing a lone hand. If you get a bad result, for whatever reason, he will blame you – and he will be right to do so.

But deception as a defender is easier for the reason that declarer is watching your cards and assuming they mean something, because defence is by its very nature a dialogue rather than a monologue. You know you have an eavesdropper, so you can deliberately send a false message, so long as the damage falls on the right head.

And deception as a defender is more satisfying precisely because it is more risky; the fact that your parcel-bomb may explode before it leaves your hands adds the spice of danger to the affair – and we all know that forbidden fruits are more fun.

Before we start to look at deception in detail I should point out that it would be good tactics before attempting any deception in defence to ask yourself the question from the World War II posters, 'Is your journey really necessary?' If declarer is not going to succeed in his contract, try to avoid complicating the issue! And deception for its own sake, when you have no clearly defined purpose in mind is on balance not a great idea. It is not that such deception cannot or will not work; the problem is that it starts to break up partnership trust. The next time you reach a congruent position and play a true card your partner will have that nagging doubt at the back of his mind.

Let me give you an example; when defending a suit contract and your partner's lead at trick one is in a suit in which you have the king and jack, then it is frequently good technique to play the jack to discover who has the queen. Well maybe not the first, but the second time that partner underleads an ace in this sort of position, won't you have a knot of tension as you make the correct technical play?

Having issued that warning, I invite you to step into the Garden of Delights – adults only.It is not an easy task to categorise areas of deception in defence, but I have tried to identify four main sub-headings, namely leading, signalling, following suit, and discarding.

One other minor point; bridge is an especially chauvinistic game, but I have done my best not to add to the sexism so prevalent in the game. Throughout this book I have used the male pronoun except where on real hands I have known that a participant was female; the masculine should be taken to include the feminine wherever relevant.

Barry Rigal 1997

1
DECEPTION ON LEAD

4th Highest or 5th?

If we assume that our partnership is playing a system of opening leads which includes fourth highest from holdings that include an honour, then it is obviously possible to vary that in two ways. You can lead from a five card suit and pretend that you have only a four card suit – or you can try and make a four card suit look longer than it is. Neither of these ploys is guaranteed to achieve anything, but sometimes you can speculate with some accuracy that this sort of deception may be relevant.

Game All. Dealer West. Teams.

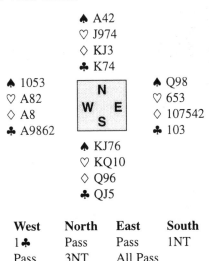

```
                      ♠ A42
                      ♡ J974
                      ◇ KJ3
                      ♣ K74
        ♠ 1053                      ♠ Q98
        ♡ A82          N            ♡ 653
        ◇ A8       W       E        ◇ 107542
        ♣ A9862        S            ♣ 103
                      ♠ KJ76
                      ♡ KQ10
                      ◇ Q96
                      ♣ QJ5
```

West	North	East	South
1♣	Pass	Pass	1NT
Pass	3NT	All Pass	

If you lead the six of clubs, then declarer is likely to knock out the ace of hearts, and then realise that the defence may well have five tricks if he concedes a trick to the ace of diamonds. Consequently, he may gamble on finding a 3-3 spade split with the queen well placed. All very unlikely but, on this layout, it will be his lucky day, not yours. However, the lead of the club two at trick one may well persuade him simply to knock out the side-suit aces, because he believes that you will only have one long club to cash. Of course, you will have to be careful to lead a small club when you are in with the ace of hearts so as not to reveal the position

Sometimes the reverse position applies – it may be to your advantage to suggest a long suit when you do not have one. For example, if you change the defensive hands in the above example, it would not be absurd to lead the club six from:

♠ Q53
♡ A82
◇ A83
♣ A962

Who knows – if clubs are 4-3-3-3 round the table maybe declarer will be so worried about the club split that he will take an unnecessary spade finesse into your hand?

It is also worth noting that varying the choice of lead on both the above examples is a relatively safe strategy. As the hand on lead clearly has most of the defensive strength, there is much less chance of creating costly confusion for your partner.

Another example of this approach – on a very different sort of hand – decided the placings in the last round of a top American Pairs event.

Game All. Pairs.

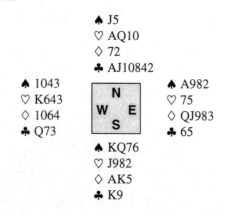

     ♠ J5
     ♡ AQ10
     ◇ 72
     ♣ AJ10842

♠ 1043   ♠ A982
♡ K643   ♡ 75
◇ 1064   ◇ QJ983
♣ Q73   ♣ 65

     ♠ KQ76
     ♡ J982
     ◇ AK5
     ♣ K9

Almost the entire field reached 3NT by South after a strong no trump opening bid, and received the lead of the heart three. Because they knew the lead was from a four card suit they figured that West was not especially distributional, and thus at least as likely as East to hold the club queen. Thus they made 11 tricks without breathing hard.

A top-rank US international was playing the contract of 3NT in front of the TV cameras (the major National US tournaments have a Vu-graph and commentary for the spectators). He received the fourth highest lead of the four of hearts, and adroitly worked out that West's probable five card suit made East favourite to hold the club queen, so he ran the club jack from dummy. It was only an overtrick, but it made the difference between second place and fifth place.

Perhaps he should have been less trusting of his opponent, Zia Mahmood, who had deliberately selected a deceptive lead in the hopes of deflecting declarer from his normal play.

There is a follow up to this point, on a related but not identical matter. Generally when you have led from a five card suit you let partner know as soon as conveniently possible by disclosing your fifth highest card. But there are many occasions when this is not such a good idea. Sometimes it is as a matter of technique – you may want to pass a suit preference message when the count is already implicitly known.

More typical, and more relevant to this book, is the idea that by concealing your low card you can lull declarer into a false sense of security. Again it may be easier to demonstrate this in a full hand.

East/West Game. Teams.

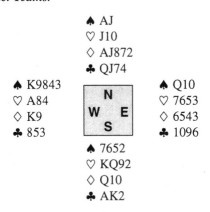

Your opponents reach 3NT after a weak no trump opening by South, and you lead the four of spades. Your partner takes the jack with his queen and returns the ten of spades. If you helpfully signal with the three then declarer will appreciate that he may have five top losers if he knocks out the heart ace – so he will take the diamond finesse on the grounds that he will probably make his contract if you have the king of diamonds and he will still survive if East has both the diamond king and ace of hearts; this way declarer comes to nine tricks without needing to test hearts.

But if you follow with the spade eight at trick two you will force declarer to show you a lot of respect if he is not simply to knock out the ace of hearts, under the assumption that the defence have no more than four top winners.

Deception of this sort is not limited to leads *up* to declarer. Positions of the following sort occur a great deal more often than most people realise.

(a)   **(b)**

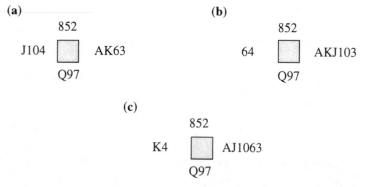

(a)

852

J104   AK63

Q97

(b)

852

64   AKJ103

Q97

(c)

852

K4   AJ1063

Q97

You can make the life of a declarer at no trumps easy, or very difficult, as East on these three holdings. South's easy plays come if you switch to the ace or three in (a), the king in (b), and the ten or jack in (c). If declarer believes the spot cards in (a) he will know the suit is 4-3, so there is no merit in ducking his queen.

In (b) declarer will score his queen on the second or third round in some comfort, and, in the third instance, declarer may try to block the suit by ducking the first trick if you switch to the ten. So what is to be done?

Well, in the first example you could try switching to the six; if South believes you have a five-card suit he might try to block the suit as in example (c) by ducking. In (b) you might try the effect of the ten on the first round – again declarer might duck to block the suit. (Mind you when declarer's holding is queen-seven doubleton you had better have your excuses ready for your partner). In (c) the effect of leading the three might persuade declarer to rise with the queen, thinking that the suit was divided 4-3 as in example (a).

There are further variations of these falsecards which are not directly count related. If declarer is known to have a guarded honour we can try to camouflage our holding even more subtly (again the play is at no trumps and you need to run your suit immediately to beat the contract).

The real holding	**Pretending to be**

	852			852	
104		AKJ63	K4		AJ1063
	Q97			Q97	

The real holding	**Pretending to be**

	852			852	
J4		AQ1063	A4(3)		QJ106(3)
	K97			K97	

In the first example the switch to the jack gives declarer an additional losing option. In the second instance you need to remain on lead so you must start with the ten, and continue with the queen so that you can cash out the suit if declarer guesses wrong on the second round too.

Coded Leads Promising or Denying Higher Honours

Many people these days find that an opening lead structure other than the top of a sequence works more efficiently. In particular the lead at no trumps of a king shows a very good suit and asks partner to unblock an honour if he has one (a holding such as AKJxx or KQ10xx might be suitable.) This system of leads also combines well with the 'strong ten', whereby you lead the ten from jack-ten or ten-nine sequences only if you have a higher honour. The jack tends to deny a higher honour from jack-ten sequences, and one leads the nine from ten-nine sequences without a higher honour.

All of this information can be very helpful to declarer too; consider the lay-out of these suits at no trumps

(a)   **(b)**

AQ4   AQ4

J10973   K8(2)   K10973   J8(2)

65(2)   65(2)

It is obvious that the coded leads (highlighted above) make life much easier for declarer. In the first example (a) he can duck the first round and take the ace on the second round. Either the king will fall or the suit will be blocked. However in (b) he can take the finesse with impunity.

However this is not entirely one-way traffic; the reason for playing this system of leads is primarily because you believe that the information you give to partner is more valuable than the information presented to declarer; but sometimes when you hold a strong enough hand you cease to need to communicate with partner – you are going to be taking all the decisions on a particular hand – and so you can make a deceptive lead within your own system. Sometimes you can predict declarer is more likely to be damaged by a false card than your partner.

The first book written on the play of the cards which has any relevance to the modern game was the work of Louis Watson. The following hand is taken from that book; since those days the false card found by Albert Morehead – a superb Bridge writer and a fine player – has become more common; but it should still catch the novice out.

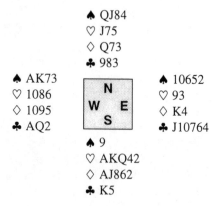

♠ QJ84
♡ J75
◇ Q73
♣ 983

♠ AK73   ♠ 10652
♡ 1086   N   ♡ 93
◇ 1095   W   E   ◇ K4
♣ AQ2   S   ♣ J10764

♠ 9
♡ AKQ42
◇ AJ862
♣ K5

West	North	East	South
–	–	–	1♡
Pass	1NT	Pass	3◊
Pass	3♡	Pass	4♡
All Pass			

Morehead sat West and heard South show a game forcing two-suiter in the red suits, and drive to game in four hearts. He led the spade king and realised that the most he could hope for from his partner was one ace or king. The problem was that any honour in the red suits would now be likely to fall, as East could hardly hold more than a doubleton in either suit. Of course partner might have the club king – but then the defence would only have two clubs to cash.

Morehead made the right initial assumption to play his partner for a top diamond, and then the right deceptive play of switching to the diamond nine! Put yourself in declarer's position; if this deceptive play had never occurred to you, would it not seem logical to you to cover the nine with dummy's queen, intending to use dummy's heart jack as an entry to repeat the finesse in diamonds to pick up the ten in East. Up went the diamond queen and down went the contract. Of course, if declarer had been left to his own devices he would have been forced to play diamonds for himself and the lack of entries to dummy would have compelled him to play East for the doubleton king, successfully.

As a general summary, you should certainly think about trying these deceptive honour leads from a sequence when you have approximately opening bid values and the opponents have bid game. It is also the case that codified leads are fairly irrelevant against slams, where the extra information is more likely to be of use to declarer than partner.

You should also be aware of the calibre of your opposition before making a falsecard lead of this sort. If your partner is watching your cards, and your opponents do not, then falsecards are worse than pointless. Conversely if your delicate attempts at passing information to your partner is the Bridge equivalent of casting Pearls before Swine, feel free to let loose with false cards at any opportunity, as there seems to be no real downside.

Underleading Aces and Other Things

The topic of underleading aces is one of the most dangerous in the whole area of deception. When it works it can be the most satisfying play in the book; when it fails it can be the most aggravating manoeuvre that your partner has ever seen!

Before we consider underleading an ace we should ask ourselves a series of questions, and we need to get a positive response to at least some of them to consider the underlead.

1. (Against a slam): has dummy promised the king, or has declarer denied a control?
2. Is there a good reason for assuming neither dummy nor declarer has a singleton – in which case underleading the ace would be more likely to cost a trick than usual?
3. Has dummy shown a very strong hand, or the equivalent of a no trump overcall, or has declarer denied a stop?
4. Has declarer shown a weak hand and implicitly not a high card in the key suit?
5. Is it likely that your partner can read the position and will not do something embarrassing on the ace underlead?

Let us look at some auctions where an ace underlead is plausible; first of all the slam auction.

West	North	East	South
–	–	Pass	1♡
Pass	3♣	Pass	3♡
Pass	4♢	Pass	5♡
Pass	6♡	All Pass	

This is an easy one. South's jump to five hearts asks North to bid slam with a spade control, so the spade suit may be distributed like this:

                    K104
          A863   [   ]   Q92
                    J75

You see what I mean about the fifth question above? There is little point in leading a low spade if your partner is going to put in the nine when declarer misguesses! You want partner to be sufficiently clued-in to think you might underlead an ace if it figured to be the right thing to do, but not to be wary of your leads in general on the grounds that you could underlead an ace at random.

Here are two hands where the underlead of an ace worked well, and as you can see the opening leader had a measure of safety in the ace underlead, because the lead was from the AQJ holding – which restricts partner's opportunity for error.

Game All. Teams.

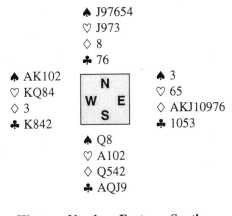

♠ J97654
♡ J973
◇ 8
♣ 76

♠ AK102
♡ KQ84
◇ 3
♣ K842

♠ 3
♡ 65
◇ AKJ10976
♣ 1053

♠ Q8
♡ A102
◇ Q542
♣ AQJ9

West	North	East	South
–	–	–	1◇ (i)
Dble	1♠	Pass	1NT
Pass	2♠	3◇	All Pass

(i)   Natural/strong no trump (2+ diamonds)

East finally got his diamond suit into the action, despite South's best efforts, in this hand from the English trials. Other tables had reached the same contract with less of a struggle.

Most tables led the spade queen against a diamond partscore and declarer made ten tricks without raising a sweat. However the lead of the club queen put East in a difficult position; perhaps his technically correct play is the king – but you can sympathise with the decision to duck, whereupon the defence took the ace of clubs and a ruff, and declarer had two more red suit losers for one down.

By contrast the next underlead was a little more dangerous, because it was quite probable that declarer was stronger than dummy: The standard result on the hand at the World Championships in Albuquerque was for East-West to make nine tricks in spades, but this was not always the case.

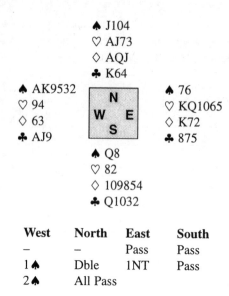

West	North	East	South
–	–	Pass	Pass
1♠	Dble	1NT	Pass
2♠	All Pass		

Marinesa Letitzia, a current US World Champion, sat North. East-West finished in two spades (East having bid one no trump at his first turn), and Marinesa selected the diamond queen as her opening salvo!

Declarer ducked, and her partner contributed the ten. Now obviously the best defence (double-dummy) is to lead a small heart, but that is a lot easier with the sight of all four hands, and Marinesa pressed on with the diamond jack, and declarer ducked again. A discomfited declarer ruffed the diamond ace, and led a heart to the queen, and a club to the nine and king.

This was the ending:

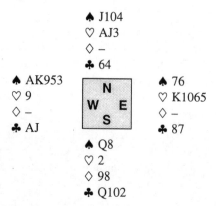

Marinesa led the ace of hearts and a small heart which her partner ruffed with the spade queen, and declarer discarded the jack of clubs. Now came the nine of diamonds, ruffed with the nine of spades and over-ruffed with the ten. Now a fourth round of hearts, ruffed with the eight of spades, provided declarer with the ultimate indignity of a third defensive uppercut for two down!

It is interesting how many times players who have underled an ace successfully try going to the well one more time, and frequently that is once too often – at least in theory.

The players generally reason that if declarer has got it wrong the first time he will do so next time too ... and they are generally right!

East/West Game. Pairs.

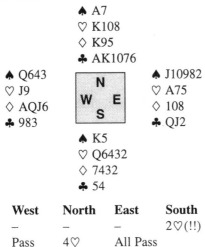

```
                ♠ A7
                ♡ K108
                ◇ K95
                ♣ AK1076
  ♠ Q643         ┌──────────┐      ♠ J10982
  ♡ J9           │    N     │      ♡ A75
  ◇ AQJ6         │  W   E   │      ◇ 108
  ♣ 983          │    S     │      ♣ QJ2
                └──────────┘
                ♠ K5
                ♡ Q6432
                ◇ 7432
                ♣ 54
```

West	North	East	South
–	–	–	2♡(!!)
Pass	4♡	All Pass	

If you have been brought up to believe that a weak two bid should be a sound six card suit, the South opening may give you apoplexy; even the excuse of it being Pairs, and your being non-vulnerable against vulnerable would cut no ice with me. But as you can see, the cards lie very invitingly for declarer.

However, the expert West on lead, Jeff Wolfson, unerringly selected the diamond queen as his opening salvo; with declarer very unlikely to hold the diamond king this has a lot going for it. Anyway declarer not unreasonably ducked this, and Wolfson could have beaten the contract trivially by playing ace and a second diamond (and a spade switch would also have worked out fine); but not unreasonably he continued with the diamond jack – now declarer could have made his contract by playing the king – but he had not come this far to get the suit right!

You can also consider the underlead of an ace (at trick one, and in mid-hand) from AQx when dummy is likely to hold the king. Perhaps you can find this sort of lay-out.

K754

AQ82 ▢ J96

103

If the queen holds, try a low one and see what happens.

The other deceptive form of underlead comes when you choose to underlead a sequence of honours, rather than to lead a card from that sequence. Typically this happens when your Left Hand Opponent has bid the suit in question and the contract finishes up in no trumps, so there is an implication that your partner may be able to contribute a card to help you out.

Here is a typical example, the defender in the West seat being Tim Seres of Australia.

A1085

KQJ72 ▢ 96

43

Tim led a low club at trick one when dummy had made its initial response in that suit and was not disappointed with the result when declarer played the eight from dummy.

A former team-mate of mine found a similar play when he had a hand with only one side entry, and decided to attack dummy's first bid suit in a contract of 3NT.

KQ743

J10985 ▢ A6

2

If he had led the jack initially then declarer would have worked out how dangerous the suit might be for the defence; but on a small card-lead it appears that you can play the queen from dummy. Even if this loses to the ace, so long as this exact position does not exist you can always duck the next round and prevent the defence from setting up four tricks in the suit.

Again, another position where you might consider an unnatural lead is through declarer's suit. A recently reported example of a successful underlead in dummy's suit featured the lead of the ten at trick one with this lay-out.

```
              J763
AKQ108       [   ]       94
               52
```

In similar vein you might consider an underlead of an ace-king-queen, or a non-standard honour lead in a suit implicitly bid by dummy with this sort of lay-out.

```
              J542
AKQ93        [   ]       108
               76
```

Do not be afraid to look stupid in these positions; the good thing about the underlead is that it will give someone a story – you just hope it is your side and not the opposition!

There are other positions in which you may underlead a sequence of honours. Consider this lay-out at no trumps.

```
              53
84           [   ]       KQ1092
              AJ76
```

If East is on lead and switches to a top honour, declarer gets his two tricks before the defence can take more than one trick. But if East switches to the ten, declarer may judge that his best play is to rise with the ace, as if he finesses he may set up three defensive winners. If the suit is blocked, with West holding a doubleton honour, then this would be the best play – but not here. Of course East may get in again and try the nine the next time if he needs three quick tricks in the suit – to fool declarer twice in the same suit has an added piquancy, but it helps to be bigger than the opponent you take for a ride in this way.

The American Internationals Jordan and Robinson showed a variant, in a position where, unusually, both halves of the defence played their part.

```
            84
953       [    ]       AKJ102
            Q76
```

When the Argentinian declarer reached 3NT (with nine top tricks outside the danger suit), Robinson led the three in his partner's suit – perhaps partly to suggest three cards, but also planting a seed of doubt in declarer's mind as to whether he had a top honour. Jordan won the ace to return the jack, and declarer elected to duck, hoping to block the suit. Again one can question declarer's play, but the fact remains that if you give declarer a chance to err he will do so, sooner or later.

Leading or Switching to Shortage

There are many occasions on opening lead where you would like to present declarer with a false description of your hand; there could be a whole host of reasons for wanting to do this – but in this section we are going to focus on simulating a lead from shortage, or not leading the standard card.

Again there are some reasons which are closer to technique (albeit fairly advanced technique) for these plays. Sometimes you may want to lead low from a doubleton if you have an entryless hand and expect that leading the top of a doubleton may cause partner problems.

Say you are on lead to 3NT, with the only honour in your hand being in partner's suit; in either of these two following positions a low card might be right – but it helps if partner knows you might do this.

(a)   **(b)**

```
          AK9                                A105
J2      [    ]      Q8643          Q2      [    ]      J9643
          1075                               K87
```

Even if you have a slightly better hand it might be right to lead low from Qx in your partner's suit where your RHO has overcalled one no trump. Assuming your partner has enough entries, this one should work well.

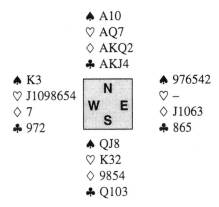

	1095	
Q2		A8643
	KJ7	

The low card lead should save a trick and a tempo for the defence.

One of the most typical plays is to pretend that you have a singleton by underleading a king. The following hand was perpetrated against my team-mates in the final of a National event.

North/South Game.

	♠ A10 ♡ AQ7 ◇ AKQ2 ♣ AKJ4	
♠ K3 ♡ J1098654 ◇ 7 ♣ 972	N W E S	♠ 976542 ♡ – ◇ J1063 ♣ 865
	♠ QJ8 ♡ K32 ◇ 9854 ♣ Q103	

North-South seem destined to make six diamonds, and our team-mates duly reached that contract via a slightly rustic route; West opened three hearts, North doubled for take-out, and South bid four diamonds, raised to six diamonds. Unfortunately the man on lead was a wily Polish player, with a name so complex that he was known to the whole world as 'Zed', that being as close as anyone could get to pronouncing his name. Zed led a low spade, and my team mate reasonably enough was more worried about the spade ruff than about the 4-1 diamond split, so he rose with the ace.

There are many situations where the lead of dummy's first bid suit will discourage declarer from taking a finesse, or will persuade him to take a ruffing finesse later on. A couple of possible distributions of the key suit.

	AQ10942				AQ10942	
K73		J6		K73		865
	85				J	

In the first example declarer may be unwilling to finesse and lose the first two tricks; he may play for some alternative chance instead. In the second example declarer is likely to play your partner for the king by taking a ruffing finesse, instead of trying to drop the king in three rounds. The lead of the seven caters for the chance that declarer may ruff one round before taking the finesse – then you will follow with what seems to be a doubleton.

Sometimes you could simulate a singleton when you have in fact got an unusual trump holding; by faking a singleton you may achieve instant gratification (as in Zed's example) or you may persuade declarer away from his best play in the trump suit because of his fear of an impending ruff.

Two possible examples of the lay-out of the trump suit are as follows:

	AJ964				A1074	
KQ3		–		QJ92		6
	108752				K853	

In the first instance declarer would make the standard safety play of leading up to dummy's jack, but if you appear to have a side-suit singleton declarer may be chary of trying the play. Similarly if declarer thinks you are about to get a ruff he may play the second suit by laying down the ace and king, rather than playing the king and small to the ten.

The opportunity of representing yourself to have a singleton is not limited to trick one. The following hand came up in the final of the Brighton Teams (the biggest single venue event in England).

North/South Game. Teams.

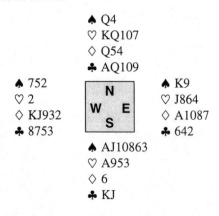

```
                    ♠ Q4
                    ♡ KQ107
                    ◇ Q54
                    ♣ AQ109
        ♠ 752               ♠ K9
        ♡ 2          N      ♡ J864
        ◇ KJ932    W   E    ◇ A1087
        ♣ 8753        S     ♣ 642
                    ♠ AJ10863
                    ♡ A953
                    ◇ 6
                    ♣ KJ
```

Neil Rosen, in the East seat for the eventual winners, heard his opponents explore for a slam, before coming to rest in five hearts. His partner led a diamond to the ace, and Rosen returned the spade nine. Declarer naturally rose with the ace, and could not recover from the bad heart split. (Even if you play the heart king and queen from dummy, another round of diamonds will ensure a trump loser for your side.)

This next hand decided the Qualifiers for the Venice Cup (the Women's World championships) in Yokohama in 1991. Great Britain, as it turned out, actually needed a game swing on this hand to qualify – and, as you will see, the odds were stacked against them.

East/West Game. Teams.

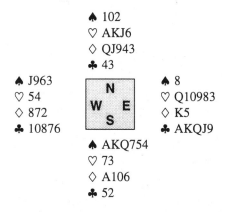

```
                    ♠ 102
                    ♡ AKJ6
                    ◇ QJ943
                    ♣ 43
    ♠ J963            N          ♠ 8
    ♡ 54                         ♡ Q10983
    ◇ 872          W   E         ◇ K5
    ♣ 10876           S          ♣ AKQJ9
                    ♠ AKQ754
                    ♡ 73
                    ◇ A106
                    ♣ 52
```

Where would you like to play the North-South cards? The Spanish played in five diamonds from the North seat, and the defence did their best by leading three rounds of clubs. To succeed, declarer must draw only two trumps and then ruff a spade, before crossing back to dummy by drawing the last trump; not difficult, you may say, but the Spanish declarer failed to get it right.

Pat Davies of Great Britain declared four spades from the South seat, after East had shown 10+ cards in hearts and clubs, and the defence also led three rounds of clubs, producing an easy +420. But how would Pat have played if the Spanish defender had cashed two clubs and switched to a diamond? If you believe East is 2-5-1-5 you might easily rise with the ace of diamonds and rely on the spades to behave. Fortunately, the defence only found this line in the post-mortem.

If you are defending a trump contract another layout which you can try to exploit is the following, in a suit bid by West:

KJ5

A10862   Q3

974

Suppose that you are on lead as East, and desperately need quick tricks in your partner's suit. Switch to the three and your partner will doubtless try to give you a ruff. On a good day declarer will finesse, hoping that your partner has no side entries; you can win the queen and hopefully put partner in via a side suit to give you your ruff.

As a general rule you could bear in mind the dual principle of forcing declarer to take a premature decision in a side-suit, before he knows how trumps will behave. In addition you should try to deceive declarer about length in a side-suit to persuade him to get his play in the trump suit wrong. If you appear to have length in a side-suit it would be natural for declarer to assume you were short in trumps, and vice versa.

So you may be able to pull the wool over declarer's eyes by simulating a low 'length' lead from a doubleton, or leading the eight or nine (which look like shortage) from an unbid five or six card suit.

Another opportunity for deceptive defence on opening lead can come when your partner has pre-empted, and you hold three cards to an honour. Let us look at this side-suit.

K6

Q42   AJ10873

95

This does not look such a dangerous suit from declarer's point of view, does it? Two quick losers but otherwise under control, one would think.

However, put yourself in the West seat; if your partner has opened a three level preempt in this suit, the lead of the queen followed by the two to the ace, will put declarer in a false position on the third round. He may ruff high unnecessarily, exposing himself to an additional trump loser.

Equally obviously this defence may give him a ruff and discard and let the contract through, so viewer discretion is advised – pick the moment to do this when you have no slow side-suit winners that may vanish to the ruff and discard.

You may think this unlikely to work in real life – however, this hand from the European championships in 1987 demonstrated that you can sometimes give declarer a problem in the easiest of contracts.

Teams.

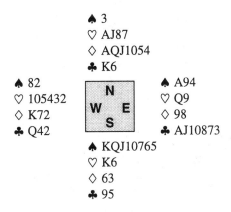

```
                 ♠ 3
                 ♡ AJ87
                 ◇ AQJ1054
                 ♣ K6
    ♠ 82                      ♠ A94
    ♡ 105432      N           ♡ Q9
    ◇ K72     W       E       ◇ 98
    ♣ Q42         S           ♣ AJ10873
                 ♠ KQJ10765
                 ♡ K6
                 ◇ 63
                 ♣ 95
```

The auction was brief – North opened one diamond, Tjolpe Flodqvist for Sweden overcalled three clubs (intermediate) and South sensibly bid four spades. P-O Sundelin, with the pile of garbage in the West seat, led the club queen for two reasons: there was the deceptive element, and the possibility of remaining on lead at the end of trick one. It worked out spectacularly well. Flodqvist won the second round of clubs and led a third round, ruffed high by declarer, who somewhat uncomfortably led a diamond to the queen, and a spade to his ten.

When no ace appeared, declarer had to decide whether Flodqvist had the doubleton or tripleton spade ace. If the former, he had to exit with a low spade, or the defence would get a trump promotion with a fourth round of clubs. Obviously the winning line on the hand is to play a top spade, but I think declarer had the percentages on his side when he played a low spade from hand, thus generating a spectacularly unlikely second trump loser.

The Portland club has just celebrated the centenary of its publishing the first rules of bridge. These days the club has been dipping its toes into serious competitive bridge, and despite handicapping itself by playing convention-free bridge (some might say this was a bonus not a disadvantage) their card play has been enough to achieve some coups. I was dummy when Richard Collins of the Portland in the West seat tried the following.

Point-a-Board.

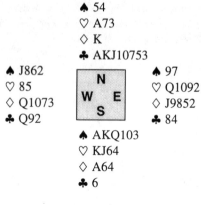

```
                    ♠ 54
                    ♡ A73
                    ◊ K
                    ♣ AKJ10753
    ♠ J862                         ♠ 97
    ♡ 85              N            ♡ Q1092
    ◊ Q1073       W     E         ◊ J9852
    ♣ Q92            S             ♣ 84
                    ♠ AKQ103
                    ♡ KJ64
                    ◊ A64
                    ♣ 6
```

West	North	East	South
–	1♣	Pass	1♠
Pass	3♣	Pass	3♡
Pass	3♠	Pass	4NT
Pass	5♡	Pass	5NT
Pass	6NT	Pass	7NT
All Pass			

I am not proud of the three spade bid, and my 6NT bid (intending to show semi-solid clubs, as with solid clubs I would have bid a grand slam) was also, as it transpired, capable of being misunderstood.

Having said that, Collins did his best to defeat what the Fates appeared to have intended as an unsportingly lucky contract, when he led the club nine at trick one. He was listening to the auction, and knew dummy, with bad spades and no great diamond stop or heart support, should have the top clubs. Unfortunately for him his reputation had gone before him, and my partner confidently finessed the clubs. A nice play by Jim Mason, and I am sure Richard would have been painfully pleased by the compliment.

The European Championships have proved an especially fertile breeding ground for deceptive play of late; of course sometimes the seed falls on stony ground.

Teams.

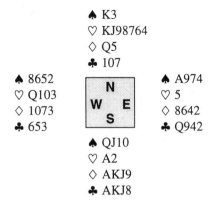

```
                    ♠ K3
                    ♡ KJ98764
                    ◇ Q5
                    ♣ 107
  ♠ 8652                         ♠ A974
  ♡ Q103          N              ♡ 5
  ◇ 1073       W     E           ◇ 8642
  ♣ 653           S              ♣ Q942
                    ♠ QJ10
                    ♡ A2
                    ◇ AKJ9
                    ♣ AKJ8
```

When Poland played Israel, the Israeli player in the North seat reached six hearts, which is comfortable on any lead but the spade ace. However Gawrys found the lead, and the Israeli declarer did not find the heart queen, and so went one down.

By contrast Marek Szymanowski for Poland played 6NT from the South seat on a spade lead to the ace, and a diamond switch. He won in hand, and played off the ace and king of hearts; when no queen appeared he fell back on the club suit, running the ten, covered by the queen and king, and then successfully playing the percentages by going back to dummy's diamond queen to play a club to the eight. 'Nicely done' you may say, but where is the deception?' Well, the point is that East could have saved the day by returning a club at trick two; declarer would never have finessed, knowing that he only needed the hearts to behave to make his contract, and by the time he misguessed the hearts it would have been too late.

I include this final hand in the section on pretending to have shortage, more because I think it is of almost unparalleled elegance than because I think you will necessarily be able to use it yourself. The perpetrator of the smash-and grab raid was Gabriel Chagas of Brazil, who has the deserved reputation of being one of the most resourceful declarers ever – together with an almost hypnotic ability to tempt his opponents into error. Look at all four hands before trying to work out how Chagas in the East seat managed to defeat four spades.

Teams.

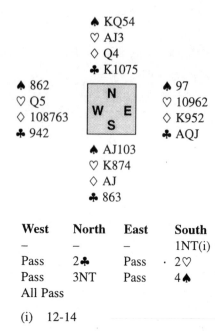

♠ KQ54
♡ AJ3
◇ Q4
♣ K1075

♠ 862
♡ Q5
◇ 108763
♣ 942

♠ 97
♡ 10962
◇ K952
♣ AQJ

♠ AJ103
♡ K874
◇ AJ
♣ 863

West	North	East	South
–	–	–	1NT(i)
Pass	2♣	Pass	· 2♡
Pass	3NT	Pass	4♠
All Pass			

(i)   12-14

West led the club two, which was conveniently ambiguous for the defence, and Chagas saw that whatever major suit honour his partner had was doomed. Deception therefore being necessary, he won the first trick with the club queen, cashed the club ace, and exited with the diamond nine! Naturally declarer won the ace, drew trumps and then took the guaranteed club finesse to dispose of his diamond loser, and Chagas produced the club jack and the diamond king to defeat the contract. It was not surprising that this sequence of plays won Chagas the award for the defence of the year.

More Count Problems

We have looked at some of the more blatant ways of confusing declarer about the defensive count in the early stages of the defence. There are however many facets to this sort of deception – for example where your intention is to deceive both declarer and partner, with the purest of intentions.

The sort of position I am envisaging comes when partner leads his suit against a no trump contract, and you win the first trick. Sometimes you need to deceive everyone in order to generate the best defence ...

North/South Game. Teams.

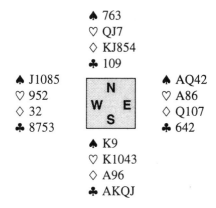

```
              ♠ 763
              ♡ QJ7
              ◇ KJ854
              ♣ 109
  ♠ J1085              ♠ AQ42
  ♡ 952       N        ♡ A86
  ◇ 32     W     E     ◇ Q107
  ♣ 8753      S        ♣ 642
              ♠ K9
              ♡ K1043
              ◇ A96
              ♣ AKQJ
```

After a straightforward auction (2NT – 3NT) your partner leads the spade jack, and you can see that there is no room for any other high card in his hand. If you return the spade two then declarer may work out that the defence have only four winners if he knocks out the heart ace. If you return the spade queen then declarer may postulate an original 5-3 split in spades, in which case he needs to take the diamond finesse, which will be the defence's fifth winner. You can of course see the converse to this; switch the diamond queen and the spade eight – so that your partner had found the same lead from:

♠ J105
♡ 952
◇ Q32
♣ 8753

Your best defence is to win the first trick and to return the spade two. Now declarer will surely knock out the ace of hearts, and allow you to cash out for one down, instead of coming home by taking the diamond finesse.

Okay, a new hand. Sometimes you want to pretend that you have three cards when you have four, for completely different reasons. Consider this hand in the contract of 3NT, at Match-point pairs, where the overtricks are of paramount significance.

East/West Game. Pairs.

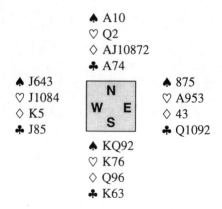

```
                    ♠ A10
                    ♡ Q2
                    ◇ AJ10872
                    ♣ A74
  ♠ J643                           ♠ 875
  ♡ J1084          N               ♡ A953
  ◇ K5        W         E          ◇ 43
  ♣ J85            S               ♣ Q1092
                    ♠ KQ92
                    ♡ K76
                    ◇ Q96
                    ♣ K63
```

When West leads the heart jack, to the queen and ace, you should pause before returning the automatic count card of the three. If you do that, declarer can see that there is no point in ducking this trick. With hearts 4-4 or 6-2 he finishes up with the same number of tricks whether he ducks or not. By contrast if you return the nine you give declarer a problem. If hearts are 5-3, a duck will allow declarer the chance to lose the diamond finesse into the safe hand. Given that some pairs will play the diamond slam, going down when the diamond finesse loses, he must be right to ensure his contract by allowing the heart nine to hold. The extra trick will make a vast difference to your score on the board – everyone else makes at least twelve tricks.

Just as on the previous hand this theory applies in reverse; let us say that the heart suit is divided:

```
                Q2
      J10854   ┌───┐   A93
              └───┘
                K76
```

and it is you who has the diamond king; now you might be able to persuade declarer to rise with the heart king on the second round of the suit if you win the ace and return the three (simulating an original 4-4 split or a 6-2 split).

Sometimes it is partner whom you want to persuade not to duck at trick two. Look at the following hand.

North/South Game. Pairs.

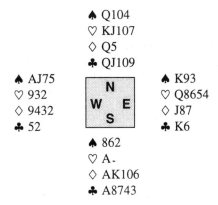

♠ Q104
♡ KJ107
◇ Q5
♣ QJ109

♠ AJ75   ♠ K93
♡ 932   ♡ Q8654
◇ 9432   ◇ J87
♣ 52   ♣ K6

♠ 862
♡ A-
◇ AK106
♣ A8743

South opens one club, and rebids a 15-17 no trump, raised to three. Your partner leads a low spade against this contract and you take the ten with the king. Again it is automatic, but a tactical error, to return the spade nine. Your partner is likely to duck this trick to preserve communications, assuming you will get in fairly quickly and he can cash out the spades. Unfortunately it will quite possibly be trick fourteen before your side gets the lead again, and you know it, from the fact that all your honours are so vulnerable. It must be right to persuade partner to win the second trick by returning the spade three; he will know that there is no point in ducking this.

Another variation on the same theme comes when you are encouraging partner to take his trick because you want him to switch to something else.

East/West Game. Pairs.

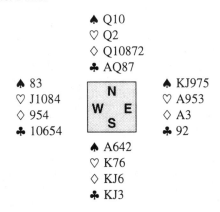

♠ Q10
♡ Q2
◇ Q10872
♣ AQ87

♠ 83   ♠ KJ975
♡ J1084   ♡ A953
◇ 954   ◇ A3
♣ 10654   ♣ 92

♠ A642
♡ K76
◇ KJ6
♣ KJ3

Your opposition reach their favourite contract of 3NT after a strong no trump opening, and the lead of the heart jack goes to the queen and ace. Try returning the nine of hearts.

If South ducks (hoping the suit is 5-3 and that your side will continue the suit), then it is up to your partner to realise that the suit is dead. If he is on good form he may overtake and switch to a spade – which will make the difference between the contract succeeding and going three down.

One final wrinkle – this hardly qualifies as deception, more a tactical manoeuvre.

North/South Game. Pairs.

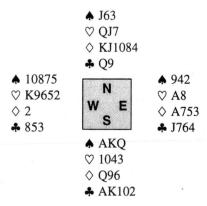

```
                    ♠ J63
                    ♡ QJ7
                    ◇ KJ1084
                    ♣ Q9
  ♠ 10875           N           ♠ 942
  ♡ K9652     W         E       ♡ A8
  ◇ 2                           ◇ A753
  ♣ 853             S           ♣ J764
                    ♠ AKQ
                    ♡ 1043
                    ◇ Q96
                    ♣ AK102
```

South opens one club and in response to North's one diamond bids 2NT to show 18-19 and North raises to 3NT. Your partner leads the heart five, playing standard fourth highest leads from good suits, and you win your ace. How do you persuade partner not to duck his heart king at trick two (in the hope that you have three hearts and an entry)?

The answer is very simple, if not entirely obvious; *don't play a heart back at trick two*. If you play a spade at trick two declarer will knock out the diamond ace, and now when you return a heart it will be too late for the hearts to set up, so your partner will have no choice but to win his heart king and hold declarer to ten tricks – rather than the eleven tricks that should result if you play a heart at trick two.

Preventing Overkill

Any play which temporarily misleads partner about your hand must technically qualify as deception – so prevention of overkill is a useful addition in one of the less discussed areas of the game. You may not even know what overkill is, but believe me, it is one of the world's most irritating experiences. Almost without exception it only occurs in defence to no trump contracts, when the defence have a complete suit to run. The critical moment generally arises at trick two of the defence, when one defender makes his correct systemic play, and creates ambiguity. Let us look at a couple of real life suit combinations which produced the overkill effect.

(a)

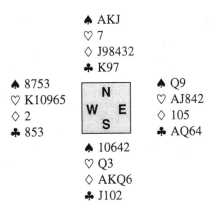

```
              ♠ AKJ
              ♡ 7
              ◇ J98432
              ♣ K97
  ♠ 8753          N        ♠ Q9
  ♡ K10965    W       E    ♡ AJ842
  ◇ 2             S        ◇ 105
  ♣ 853                    ♣ AQ64
              ♠ 10642
              ♡ Q3
              ◇ AKQ6
              ♣ J102
```

West led the six of hearts against 3NT; East won with the ace and returned the standard count card of the four. When South contributed the queen impassively, West thought the suit was divided

```
                7
     K10965  ┌────┐  A42
             └────┘
               QJ83
```

so he ducked – doubly embarrassing because it was not only a trick, it was declarer's ninth trick for his contract.

Overkill mark II ....

(b)

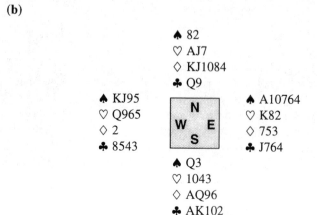

♠ 82
♡ AJ7
◇ KJ1084
♣ Q9

♠ KJ95
♡ Q965
◇ 2
♣ 8543

♠ A10764
♡ K82
◇ 753
♣ J764

♠ Q3
♡ 1043
◇ AQ96
♣ AK102

North raised a strong no trump to game, and West did well to lead a spade. East won the trick and returned the six; West took the queen with his king, and came to the conclusion that South had Q1073 and East A64, so he tried to put his partner in with a club for another spade play ....

(Notice, West was playing South quite a compliment – it would be good deceptive play as South to play the queen in this position; the rule of eleven tells you that West has the king and jack so the cards are equivalent. Also note that if East had returned the ten it would have cleared up the problem, but blocked the suit.)

What went wrong? Well the overkill phenomenon struck; East had such a good holding in his partner's suit that he could not convey it to his partner. His play at trick one was forced, and his natural count card did not do its proper job at the next turn. Let us 'rewind' and have another go at defending these hands. If we can spot the danger of overkill, perhaps we can do something about it.

On hand (a) we hold five cards in the suit partner has led – so the possibility of overkill is a live one. At the end of trick one partner appears to have five cards in the suit; we have seen that the true card return of the four gave partner a problem – he could not distinguish between a three card holding and a five-card holding. Why do we not pretend we have four cards in hearts, by returning the two? This solves all partner's problems; whether we have the jack or not, it cannot hurt to win the second trick and play the heart ten – result: happiness.

On hand (b) let us try the same thing, by returning the four, to simulate a four card suit. Partner will swallow the bait by pressing on with the suit at trick three, and the position will become plain.

Now we have identified the problem in arrears, let us see whether we can do a little forward planning.

Cover up the West and South hands, and put yourself in the East seat to see if prevention is better than cure.

East/West Game. Teams.

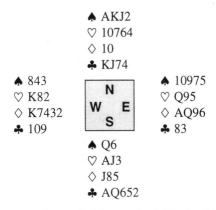

```
                    ♠ AKJ2
                    ♡ 10764
                    ◇ 10
                    ♣ KJ74
        ♠ 843           N           ♠ 10975
        ♡ K82      W        E       ♡ Q95
        ◇ K7432         S           ◇ AQ96
        ♣ 109                       ♣ 83
                    ♠ Q6
                    ♡ AJ3
                    ◇ J85
                    ♣ AQ652
```

North uses Stayman and then finishes up in 3NT after his partner opens a weak no trump. West leads the diamond three and East can see the likelihood of a five-card suit opposite. But, whatever the length of your partner's suit, there is no need to make the standard 'expert' play of the queen at trick one – if declarer wins the king it may be hard subsequently to convince West that East has this much in the suit. Simply win trick one with the ace, and return the queen not the six. This has two bonuses; first of all when partner takes the jack with the king you do not leave him guessing as to whether a heart shift is a good idea – as it would be if you had:

♠ 10975
♡ AJ95
◇ A6
♣ Q86

And the second added bonus is that occasionally you may actually need to play the queen at trick two to unblock the suit, to allow you to cash your 5 tricks in diamonds, as in the above diagram.

What we are doing, in summary, is to misrepresent our remaining holding by one card (making three look like two, or four look like three) if we can see that the effect of doing this would be to allow partner to continue happily with the suit, and that playing our true card could create an ambiguity of two (four cards looking like two, or three like one) which could be fatal to the defence.

I should emphasise at this point that in general it is a very bad idea to leave an ambiguity of one card. It is to avoid such ambiguity that some people lead third and fifth in their partner's suit. They also play low from three small in their partner's suit if they have not supported it to avoid confusion with a doubleton. But in our current examples the critical issue is that the one card confusion still allows partner to make the right play, whereas the two card confusion would not.

Preventing Declarer from Blocking Your Suits

We have looked at ways of misleading declarer and partner about the count in a critical suit, to get them to take tricks or duck them to suit our purposes. The same principle of misleading declarer also arises, relatively infrequently, when declarer has the power to block a suit, but does not or will not realise it unless you rub his nose in it.

Let us look at a single suit in isolation, and then at how this might fit into a whole hand.

```
                    7
A865(4)3   [   ]   KQ109
                 J(4)2
```

I was faced with this problem in front of the cameras when the North were playing against the South of England. Against a rather poorly bid three no trump contract my partner led the three, and it was clear from the leading methods that we played (low cards imply a good suit) that the suit could be run for at least five tricks so long as we did not block it. The embarrassing thing was that my partner could have had either five or six cards – hence the bracketed (four) above. If my partner had a five-card suit I was confident that if I won the king or queen at trick one and returned the nine South would not think of playing the jack and we could unblock the suit happily. But if declarer had the doubleton jack this would be a spectacularly stupid way to block a previously unblocked suit. Never being afraid to look idiotic, I went for the falsecard route and all was well.

But the general point is more relevant than the specific holding: do not be over-eager to cash your side's long suit; check that there are no potential problems with internal blockages.

The key give-away is when third hand has relative shortness and no low cards. It is at that point that deception becomes relevant.

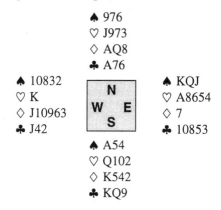

After an unopposed auction 1◇ – 1♡ – 1NT – 3NT, your partner leads the spade two and you can immediately appreciate that if your partner has four spades to the ace you can do anything you like in terms of the order you play your top spades and the contract still goes down; what you have to avoid, if partner has four spades to the ten, is declarer winning the first or second spade.

You could try the spade king at trick one and follow with the jack (which might cause partner problems if declarer for some reason wins trick one), but it looks better to play the jack at trick one followed by the queen.

Declarer will surely assume you have QJx, and play for his legitimate chance that you hold the ace and king of hearts, by ducking the second spade. But if you win trick one with the jack and follow up with the king, declarer may work out the potential blockage, and win the second spade to cross to table with a diamond and play the heart nine. (Note: this is good, and deceptive, declarer play, trying to persuade you to duck if you held ♡Axxx or ♡Kxxx, which would knock out your partner's entry while the spades are still blocked). As the cards lie, this line would actually be a legitimate way to make the contract.

Sometimes you can try to persuade declarer to unblock a suit which Nature had intended to leave blocked.

As West you win the opening lead in a side-suit at no trumps and now need to cash four tricks in this suit on the go. It is very much a matter of personal taste how you persuade declarer that you have one holding and not the other.

I think with the first holding that to lead the ten, then the jack, might suggest AJ102, which would be ideal. With the second holding I would lead the queen and then the ten (which is what I would do if I were guileless with the first holding.)

A third regularly occurring position comes when you have attacked a suit like this at trick one in no trumps.

Honest players in the first instance lead the the five to the ten and king, and then continue with the jack – sometimes allowing declarers to duck the second round and block the suit. Put yourself in declarer's position and play the second example in the same way – maybe declarer will duck here too.

One of the most elegant and unusual examples along these lines comes from an American Nationals:

North/South Game. Matchpoint Pairs.

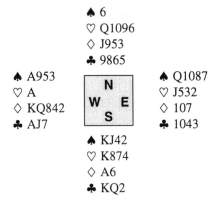

```
                    ♠ 6
                    ♡ Q1096
                    ◇ J953
                    ♣ 9865
    ♠ A953          ┌─────────┐        ♠ Q1087
    ♡ A             │    N    │        ♡ J532
    ◇ KQ842         │ W     E │        ◇ 107
    ♣ AJ7           │    S    │        ♣ 1043
                    └─────────┘
                    ♠ KJ42
                    ♡ K874
                    ◇ A6
                    ♣ KQ2
```

The auction was short and not particularly sweet from South's perspective; he opened 1NT, and West either could not make a penalty double or viewed that someone might run if he did double.

The lead of the diamond four went to the nine, ten and ace, and West won the heart ace at trick two to advance an innocent diamond eight; South's decision to duck should not be criticised too harshly; what happened in practice was that West cashed another three diamonds, squeezing South out of a heart and two spades. West unkindly exited with a low club, and declarer tested the hearts, then misguessed the spades and went three down.

Switching to Unsupported Honours

Before looking at the deceptive element of switching to an unsupported honour, it may be worth emphasising that such plays do not only deceive; sometimes these plays are also technically correct.

Sometimes it is easy to spot the position – sometimes very difficult. If the object is to reduce declarer's or dummy's trumps twice, by forcing him to ruff, then the switch to an honour may be positionally necessary. Let us look at essentially the same example, but from four different perspectives in the East seat.

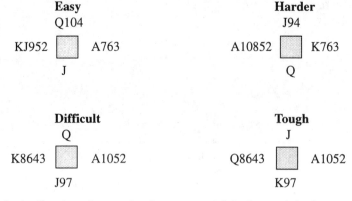

Easy
Q104
KJ952 / A763
J

Harder
J94
A10852 / K763
Q

Difficult
Q
K8643 / A1052
J97

Tough
J
Q8643 / A1052
K97

In the first 'easy' example, the presence of the long suit in dummy makes the play of the ace easy, but, in the second example, the power of the closed hand strikes again, and it is not so simple to start with the king to pin the stiff queen. Likewise in the third and fourth examples it is necessary to underlead your ace as East to force dummy to ruff twice, and the fourth example crosses into deceptiveness in that declarer can actually do something about the position if he guesses correctly.

The play of an unsupported honour is frequently made from shortage, looking for a ruff, or to kill a presumed singleton honour in declarer's hand. Sometimes however it is the only way to escape from an end-play, or to give declarer a guess as opposed to a sure thing. One example with a slight modification should show what I mean.

(a)

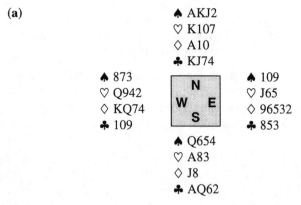

```
                    ♠ AKJ2
                    ♡ K107
                    ◇ A10
                    ♣ KJ74
   ♠ 873                        ♠ 109
   ♡ Q942           N           ♡ J65
   ◇ KQ74        W     E        ◇ 96532
   ♣ 109            S           ♣ 853
                    ♠ Q654
                    ♡ A83
                    ◇ J8
                    ♣ AQ62
```

(b)

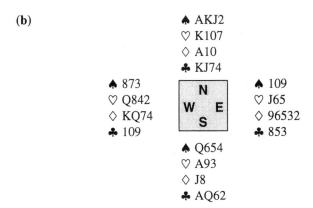

                    ♠ AKJ2
                    ♡ K107
                    ◇ A10
                    ♣ KJ74
    ♠ 873   ♠ 109
    ♡ Q842   N   ♡ J65
    ◇ KQ74   W   E   ◇ 96532
    ♣ 109   S   ♣ 853
                    ♠ Q654
                    ♡ A93
                    ◇ J8
                    ♣ AQ62

In both instances declarer plays six spades, which is a moderate contract, but only because of the mirror image of shapes of his hand and dummy. In (a), when declarer has drawn trumps and cashed off the clubs before throwing West in with a top diamond, West can beat the contract by force, by exiting with the heart queen. Now declarer can not avoid a heart loser. Contrast this with what happens if West exits with the heart nine or a small card. In (b), West gets endplayed with a diamond honour again; this time he gives declarer a losing option by exiting with the queen, anything else being hopeless. Should declarer get it right? Probably – it depends whether he thinks West is good enough to exit with an unsupported honour in this position.

Similarly, as West, you may find yourself opening up this suit.

(a)

                    J95
            K104 | | Q832
                    A76

The only chance to get two tricks is to lead the king and hope for a misguess.

(b)

                    J95
            Q104 | | A832
                    K76

But beware. Your partner may not be enormously impressed with the deceptive switch to the queen on this layout!

If you are going to be able to switch to the honour in those positions, what happens when you are West in this position:

```
              J95
        KQ4  [  ]  10832
              A76
```

I think a small card should work; declarer may assume you have Q104 or are just not good enough to underlead a king-queen.

Other suits where both East and West can present declarer with a losing option are the following:

(a)   **(b)**

```
        K93                                      K93
  AJ7  [  ]  1064                        J107  [  ]  A64
        Q852                                     Q852
```

(c)

```
              K93
        J74  [  ]  A106
              Q852
```

The shift by West to the jack has a pretty fair chance of success in (a); however if East is on lead instead, the best he can do in this position would be to try the ten, pretending to be a man with J106.

In (b) West can shift to the jack or ten, depending on the number of double-bluffs South expects him to play. By contrast East would shift to a low card, and West must rise to the occasion by playing the jack not the ten.

In (c) West must lead the jack and East must lead the ten to give the defence a chance to get two tricks.

There are a number of more obscure positions where you need to shift to an honour. In a way they all derive from the genuine technical position where East can 'surround' the ten by leading the jack initially.

```
              1042
       K983  [  ]  AJ7
              Q65
```

Now consider the following holdings; in each case you are East and need to run the suit in defence:

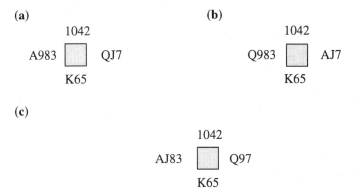

(a)

```
        1042
A983  [    ]  QJ7
        K65
```

(b)

```
        1042
Q983  [    ]  AJ7
        K65
```

(c)

```
        1042
AJ83  [    ]  Q97
        K65
```

In all these examples, you start by leading a middle honour, and continuing with a small card if you are left on lead. Declarer has no clue as to what the right winning strategy is; compare what happens if you start with a small card when you have the ace, or if declarer knows your lead of the queen would promise the jack, and the lead of the jack would deny the queen!

Are these plays too difficult to find at the table? Well, I suppose it depends who you are ... When this hand came up in the Macallan *Sunday Times* Invitation pairs event, two different players in the East seat found the switch to the same unsupported honour.

Game All. Teams.

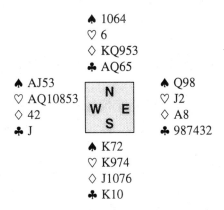

```
                ♠ 1064
                ♡ 6
                ◇ KQ953
                ♣ AQ65
♠ AJ53                      ♠ Q98
♡ AQ10853    N             ♡ J2
◇ 42       W   E           ◇ A8
♣ J           S            ♣ 987432
                ♠ K72
                ♡ K974
                ◇ J1076
                ♣ K10
```

South was declarer in both instances, in one case in the sensible contract of three diamonds, in the other case in the silly contract of 2NT.

Against three diamonds the opening lead was the club jack. Declarer won the king and played the diamond jack. Zia Mahmood in the East seat realised that, if his side took their club ruff, declarer would hold his spade losers to one, by throwing spades on dummy's clubs. His only hope was the position shown: he switched to the spade queen, and declarer ducked, expecting Zia to have the queen jack of spades; now the defence have the choice of taking a club ruff or playing a second spade to get their fifth trick.

In 2NT you appear to be going two down – an insignificant loss as the par contract is your opponents taking nine tricks in hearts. However, the opening lead was a small heart, and South won his heart king. On the jack of diamonds West, Cezary Balicki of Poland, played the two (saying 'I am happy for you to switch') and his partner Adam Zmudzinski duly won the second diamond to play the spade queen. Again declarer innocently ducked, and the roof fell in – he lost five hearts, four spades and the diamond ace for five down.

Sometimes you need to switch to an honour to simulate a different sort of sequence. Again let us postulate play in no trumps, and that you are East. If you know from the bidding that your partner's shape and high cards are limited, you may need to resort to desperate measures ....

The real position			**Pretending to be**		
	J93			J93	
Q1064		K82	864		KQ102
	A75			A75	

If you switch to the king you force declarer to take an immediate view as to what is going on. If you play a small card the defence has no chance.

Ruffage Problems

It is normal practice to give partner the ruff he appears to want, when he leads from shortage. However, sometimes this is not a good idea especially if you know that he will not be able to over-ruff, which may simultaneously expose your delicate trump holding. This hand came up in the European Championships in Turku in 1989, and features a fine play by declarer as well as the defence.

Game All. Teams.

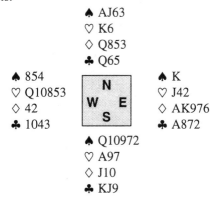

```
              ♠ AJ63
              ♡ K6
              ◇ Q853
              ♣ Q65
♠ 854                        ♠ K
♡ Q10853      N              ♡ J42
◇ 42        W   E            ◇ AK976
♣ 1043        S              ♣ A872
              ♠ Q10972
              ♡ A97
              ◇ J10
              ♣ KJ9
```

North-South reached four spades after a nebulous diamond opening, and West led the diamond four. East intelligently observed that if he played a third round of diamonds West's inability to over-ruff declarer would clear up any guess for declarer in trumps, so he switched to a heart after two rounds of diamonds. Unfortunately declarer was alive to the possibility himself, and so he cautiously won the heart in dummy, and ruffed a diamond back to hand himself with the spade ten! Now West's failure to over-ruff made the position crystal-clear, and declarer duly dropped East's singleton king.

It is rarer, but not all that unusual, for the defence to be able to give one ruff, but not to want to give a second ruff. To achieve success in this sort of position may require some fancy footwork – and arguably this hand belongs in the deceptive signalling rather than the leading category.

East/West Game. Dealer North. Matchpoint Pairs.

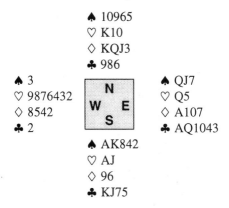

```
              ♠ 10965
              ♡ K10
              ◇ KQJ3
              ♣ 986
♠ 3                          ♠ QJ7
♡ 9876432     N              ♡ Q5
◇ 8542      W   E            ◇ A107
♣ 2           S              ♣ AQ1043
              ♠ AK842
              ♡ AJ
              ◇ 96
              ♣ KJ75
```

West	North	East	South
–	Pass	1♣	1♠
Pass	3◇	Pass	4♠
All Pass			

North's jump to three diamonds showed the values for a raise to three spades and a good diamond suit, and West led his singleton club against four spades. East's dilemma is that he wants to give partner his club ruff, win the diamond ace, and play a fourth round of clubs. But West's failure to ruff with a high trump will then tip off South as to how to play trumps.

It must be better to try something devious. Two options – though neither is guaranteed to succeed. You could cash the club ace, and then give your partner a ruff with the club ten. This is a suit preference for the higher suit, and your partner will dutifully play a heart; on a good day, declarer may sigh with relief and play trumps from the top.

Perhaps a less blatant way to defend is to lay down the diamond ace at trick two, and only then to give partner a ruff. Now there is no re-entry to your hand, and South has to work out why you 'misdefended' – to me this looks less like an attempt to pull the wool over his eyes.

Refraining from the Cash-out

This is a relatively simple concept which really only has one variation. Occasionally, it may be to your advantage not to cash the established long card in your partner's suit. It may tempt declarer into an indiscretion.

Game All. Pairs.

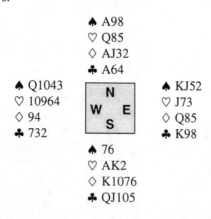

```
              ♠ A98
              ♡ Q85
              ◇ AJ32
              ♣ A64
  ♠ Q1043      N        ♠ KJ52
  ♡ 10964   W     E     ♡ J73
  ◇ 94         S        ◇ Q85
  ♣ 732                 ♣ K98
              ♠ 76
              ♡ AK2
              ◇ K1076
              ♣ QJ105
```

South opens a weak no trump, raised to 3NT, and West finds the spade lead. You have the opportunity for two fine defensive plays. To start with you win the first trick with the king and return the jack, simulating a three card spade suit, then exit with the spade five to dummy's ace. Declarer crosses to hand in hearts for the club finesse and you win and exit with a heart. Declarer could cash nine tricks now – but, playing pairs, wouldn't you be tempted to take the diamond finesse into the safe hand for an overtrick?

North/South Game. Teams.

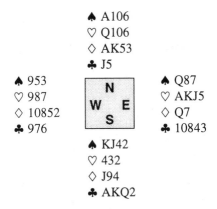

```
                    ♠ A106
                    ♡ Q106
                    ◊ AK53
                    ♣ J5
   ♠ 953          ┌──────────┐      ♠ Q87
   ♡ 987          │    N     │      ♡ AKJ5
   ◊ 10852        │  W   E   │      ◊ Q7
   ♣ 976          │    S     │      ♣ 10843
                  └──────────┘
                    ♠ KJ42
                    ♡ 432
                    ◊ J94
                    ♣ AKQ2
```

South opens a 14-16 no trump, raised to three. Your partner finds his best lead for a decade, kicking off with the heart nine. You win and cash two more hearts only, giving declarer the impression that West has the long heart. (As the cards lie if you cash the last heart declarer will test diamonds before looking for the spade queen, making nine tricks trivially.) When you exit with a club, it would take a superhuman declarer to avoid taking a spade finesse into the safe hand, and the last heart will come as a rude surprise.

Giving Declarer a Losing Option

Most people will give you credit for not being a complete fool – some of the time. Frequently however you can leave declarer unsure of whether your inferior play has been designed to generate an attractive, but losing, alternative – or whether you truly are stupid. If they play you for the latter possibility, it is the kind of insult that will carry its own reward with it – and they may not be so insulting the second time around.

For our first example you may care to put yourself in the East seat, and cover up the West and South hands.

Game All. Teams.

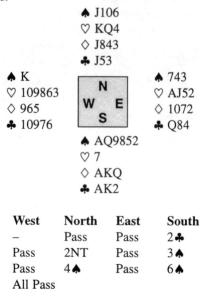

	♠ J106	
	♡ KQ4	
	◇ J843	
	♣ J53	

West	North	East	South
–	Pass	Pass	2♣
Pass	2NT	Pass	3♠
Pass	4♠	Pass	6♠
All Pass			

Your partner leads the heart ten, to the king and your ace, as declarer follows with the seven. Dummy is satisfyingly bare – any thoughts as to where to go for honey?

Look at it this way: if declarer has solid spades, you are giving nothing away by playing a heart back – declarer always had at least one entry to dummy via the spade jack. But if declarer is missing a trump honour you can see that he may not be able to reach dummy; why not help him to take a losing finesse? If you look at the full hand you can see that left to his own devices declarer has little option but to lay down the spade ace, with what from your perspective would be regicidal consequences. So help him in a different direction.

Another sort of holding where you can assist declarer to self-destruct is the following:

```
              K63
   Q       ┌──────┐      9852
           └──────┘
            AJ1074
```

Again, if declarer is not given a helping hand he would probably get this trump suit right, by leading to the king before taking the finesse. But if

East plays the suit first, by leading a small card, declarer may well take advantage of a not so free finesse. If he puts in the ten he creates a loser where the Fates had intended none.

The Matlock congress would not necessarily be the place that you would look at first, in order to find a duel between two of Britain's finest junior players. However, in 1977, two of the (then) under-26 players from Cambridge came face-to-face.

East/West Game. Pairs.

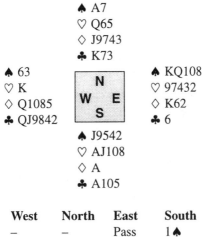

```
              ♠ A7
              ♡ Q65
              ◇ J9743
              ♣ K73
  ♠ 63                      ♠ KQ108
  ♡ K         N            ♡ 97432
  ◇ Q1085   W   E          ◇ K62
  ♣ QJ9842    S            ♣ 6
              ♠ J9542
              ♡ AJ108
              ◇ A
              ♣ A105
```

West	North	East	South
–	–	Pass	1♠
Pass	1NT	Pass	2♡
Pass	2♠	All Pass	

Richard Granville in the South seat took a fairly restrained view, after his partner had been similarly pessimistic, so his side were already going to get a good match-point score. However the play was all about over-tricks. Graham Kirby led the club queen, and Granville won the ace, and played two rounds of spades. John Armstrong in the East seat took this trick and decided to shift to the diamond king (which would have been right if declarer had the singleton queen) and Granville took his ace, to play a club to the king, which Armstrong ruffed, to play a second diamond.

Declarer threw his losing club, and Kirby won his queen and played a third club, which Granville ruffed.

This was the ending:

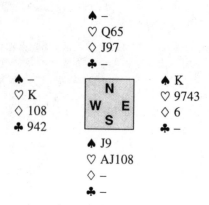

Granville exited with a third spade to Armstrong, who played a heart perforce. After some thought Granville played the ace, and dropped the singleton king. The reason for this play was that he respected Armstrong as a defender enough to know that if John had had the heart king he would have cashed his spade winner when he was last on lead. If he had allowed himself to be endplayed, it was because it was to his advantage to be left to open up the hearts – hence he could not have the king.

2
DECEPTION
IN SIGNALLING

While it is relatively clear that deception on lead must involve play by the hand who is first to play to a trick, the difference between deceptive signalling and deception in following suit may not be clear. I have created a possibly artificial distinction by defining the signal as a card whose sole purpose is ostensibly to convey information to partner, as opposed to a play where you are simply following suit, or trying to win the trick.

False Count

It is standard practice to tell your partner that you have a doubleton in a suit in which he leads the ace (from ace-king) by playing a high-low. This is not always the right defence, if in practice you do not want partner to lead a third round of the suit. Let us look at some examples of why you should leave partner under the impression that you have three cards in the critical suit.

First, an obvious one! You have no trumps to ruff the third round of the suit. Unlikely, you say – well, this hand came up a week before I write these words; it was played at 16 tables in the North American Swiss Teams Finals.

East/West Game. Teams.

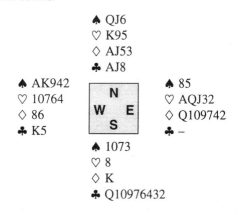

```
                  ♠ QJ6
                  ♡ K95
                  ◇ AJ53
                  ♣ AJ8
   ♠ AK942                      ♠ 85
   ♡ 10764        N             ♡ AQJ32
   ◇ 86        W     E          ◇ Q109742
   ♣ K5           S             ♣ –
                  ♠ 1073
                  ♡ 8
                  ◇ K
                  ♣ Q10976432
```

After a 1NT (15-17) no trump opening from North, East overcalled two clubs to show hearts and a minor. There are no text-books which tell you how to handle the South hand, so South simply jumped to five clubs, doubled by West. This was the normal contract, although on a good day you might make five hearts.

On the lead of a top spade many Easts fell from grace and played the eight. West tried to give his partner a ruff, and declarer now had no problems in getting the trumps right, and discarding the heart loser on the diamond ace. Where East sensibly did not show his doubleton, West switched to a heart, and the defence then cashed a second spade and tried to cash another heart. I reckon that declarer should get the trumps right on the auction, to escape for one down – but can you see how declarer can clear up the problem (as the cards lie) without having to guess? You know that East either has three spades, or no clubs; so ruff the second heart, overtake the diamond king with the ace, and play a third round of spades. When East discards it is clear he has a void in clubs.

On this next deal when you hold the West hand there is scope for good defensive play. North plays in four spades doubled.

East/West Game. Pairs.

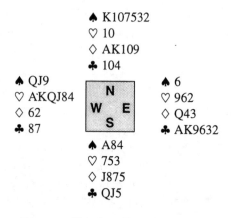

```
              ♠ K107532
              ♡ 10
              ◇ AK109
              ♣ 104
  ♠ QJ9                     ♠ 6
  ♡ AKQJ84       N          ♡ 962
  ◇ 62        W     E       ◇ Q43
  ♣ 87           S          ♣ AK9632
              ♠ A84
              ♡ 753
              ◇ J875
              ♣ QJ5
```

West	North	East	South
–	–	Pass	Pass
1♡	1♠	2♣	2♠
3♡	3♠	4♡	Pass
Pass	4♠	Dble	All Pass

When East leads a top club against four spades, it can do no harm to discourage the suit, as you know that at best getting a ruff will break even; as you can see, if East goes ahead and gives his partner a ruff it will allow North to discard the heart loser. Of course East might cash the second top club, in case West has a singleton club, but the position at the end of the second round of the suit should be clear. If partner has a doubleton and does not want a ruff, he has his reasons – don't try to over-rule him!

There are a couple of other good reasons for not telling the truth with your initial signal. Let us look at why you should tell partner you like his opening lead, even when you are not mad about it.

First of all there may be no better lead available; let us look at where we want to prevent partner making the 'obvious' switch.

East/West Game.

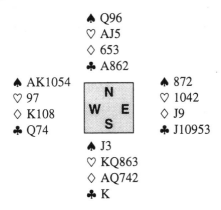

```
              ♠ Q96
              ♡ AJ5
              ◇ 653
              ♣ A862
♠ AK1054                      ♠ 872
♡ 97          N               ♡ 1042
◇ K108      W   E             ◇ J9
♣ Q74         S               ♣ J10953
              ♠ J3
              ♡ KQ863
              ◇ AQ742
              ♣ K
```

Playing a five card major system South opens one heart, West overcalls one spade, North bids two spades to show at least a three heart invitation and South bids four hearts. When West leads a top spade your systemic play would be the two, but do you really want partner to play a diamond, which is his most probable switch if you discourage spades?

You are better off encouraging a spade continuation (before the mice get at it) and allowing partner to collect his diamond winners in the fullness of time.

Well if it can be fun to deceive partner into doing the right thing, it is obviously more fun to bamboozle declarer into doing the wrong thing. What this generally involves is trying to persuade declarer that you are short enough in partner's suit that you are threatening a ruff or over-ruff.

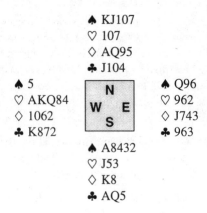

♠ KJ107
♡ 107
◇ AQ95
♣ J104

♠ 5
♡ AKQ84
◇ 1062
♣ K872

♠ Q96
♡ 962
◇ J743
♣ 963

♠ A8432
♡ J53
◇ K8
♣ AQ5

After South, your left-hand opponent opens one spade your opponents reach game in that denomination, despite your partner's two heart overcall. When your partner leads a top heart, much your best chance of defeating the contract is to signal a high-low in hearts to simulate a doubleton. If your partner leads three rounds of the suit, do you think declarer will be able to bring himself to ruff low? If he ruffs high then you have a trump trick and a club to come.

(Note that declarer has an elegant line to make if you tell the truth in hearts. Say your partner leads three rounds of hearts and declarer ruffs low; then he wins the spade king, cashes three rounds of diamonds finishing in dummy, discarding a club from hand, and then runs the spade jack. This line succeeds so long as West started with either one or two spades.)

The play of simulating a doubleton can generate remarkable results, even when you do not appear to have a vestige of a trump trick. Let us say that you make the same strong encouragement in hearts when the trump suit of spades is dealt as follows:

KQ109

J5   76

A8432

Declarer ruffs the third heart high, notices your third heart with grave suspicion, and then has to find the spade jack to make his contract – and he may well assume that your defensive deception was based on holding trump length, such as three trumps to the jack.

The European Championship is perhaps the best venue to see top-class teams meeting; there is a fortnight of bridge at which one can see the best players matching wits. On the following hand between France and Poland, the Poles came off best, when one player helped to promote his partner's trumps.

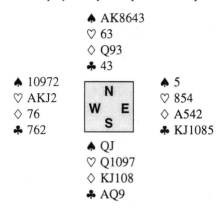

```
                    ♠ AK8643
                    ♡ 63
                    ◇ Q93
                    ♣ 43
   ♠ 10972                        ♠ 5
   ♡ AKJ2          N              ♡ 854
   ◇ 76         W     E           ◇ A542
   ♣ 762           S              ♣ KJ1085
                    ♠ QJ
                    ♡ Q1097
                    ◇ KJ108
                    ♣ AQ9
```

When South opened a 15-17 no trump North transferred into spades and bid four spades. Moszczynski (all the best Polish players have at least one Z in their name I thought – but maybe his partner, Julian Klukowski, has one in his middle name) led the heart ace. Put yourself in Klukowski's shoes for a simple piece of mental arithmetic; partner has at least seven points in hearts, you are looking at eight points, dummy has nine points and declarer has 15-17 points.

Partner therefore has at most a side-suit jack, and therefore your club king is dead. Your best chance to get the setting trick (to go with your three top red winners) is to mislead everyone at the table into thinking you only have two hearts.

A third round of hearts may persuade declarer to ruff high in dummy – in which case you may get a trump trick or conceivably a trick with the diamond jack, to which Fate had not entitled you.

Of course real life does not always work out equitably, but on this occasion the cards co-operated perfectly. Declarer had no reason to disbelieve the defence; he ruffed the third heart high in dummy, thereby generating a loser for himself, and going one down.

Sometimes, by contrast, you want to persuade declarer that there is no defensive ruff threatened, so that he misjudges how to deal with the trump suit.

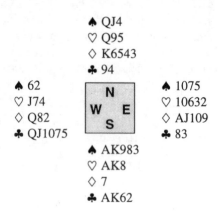

♠ QJ4
♡ Q95
◇ K6543
♣ 94

♠ 62   N   ♠ 1075
♡ J74   W   E   ♡ 10632
◇ Q82   S   ◇ AJ109
♣ QJ1075   ♣ 83

♠ AK983
♡ AK8
◇ 7
♣ AK62

Your opponents reach an excellent six spade contract, the club queen is led, and declarer sees that he can make either with the diamond king well placed or if something favourable happens in clubs. He wins the opening lead and plays a diamond to the king and ace. You exit with a heart, and declarer wins in dummy and plays a club to his king. Now is the moment of truth; if you started a peter in clubs a declarer on good form might come home by ruffing two clubs high in dummy and finessing the spade nine. However, if you simply followed up the line in clubs declarer will surely ruff the third club low, and get over-ruffed.

There is also a relatively rare position where you can see that declarer at no trumps may have the problem of deciding how many rounds to hold up in partner's suit. Say West opens a weak two spades (systemically either a five or six-card suit) and South finishes up in 3NT. When partner leads the king, showing a suit with three honours, and asking you to give count – this is the lay-out:

J5

KQ1086   972

A43

If you show an odd number it is easy for declarer to hold up to the third round. but if you play high-low to show an even number it is unlikely that declarer will hold up twice.

Our final example is, I think, rather a difficult one to find; perhaps it is because your natural feeling of exasperation at partner's choice of opening lead might distract you from the best defence.

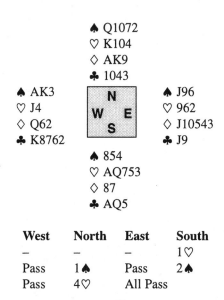

♠ Q1072
♡ K104
◇ AK9
♣ 1043

♠ AK3
♡ J4
◇ Q62
♣ K8762

♠ J96
♡ 962
◇ J10543
♣ J9

♠ 854
♡ AQ753
◇ 87
♣ AQ5

West	North	East	South
–	–	–	1♡
Pass	1♠	Pass	2♠
Pass	4♡	All Pass	

You may not agree with South's or North's rebid (as North I would rather rebid a forcing three hearts) but the net result is that you get to defend four hearts, and your partner leads the spade ace, thus clearing up a guess for declarer that he would no doubt have got wrong.

If you make the straightforward, honest, play of the six, then declarer will eventually play a spade to the queen and bring in the spades for two tricks. If you peter in spades your partner will try to give you a ruff at trick three, and declarer will surely finesse the ten, hoping simply to find you with the club king, in which case the third club eventually goes on the spade queen. Not this time.

Sometimes a signal can blatantly give declarer a losing option – you may consider declarer was rather gullible given that the defenders here were one of the strongest pairs in the world, Bjorn Fallenius and Mats Nilsland of Sweden.

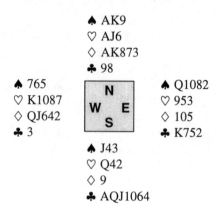

```
              ♠ AK9
              ♡ AJ6
              ◇ AK873
              ♣ 98
♠ 765                        ♠ Q1082
♡ K1087      N               ♡ 953
◇ QJ642    W   E             ◇ 105
♣ 3          S               ♣ K752
              ♠ J43
              ♡ Q42
              ◇ 9
              ♣ AQJ1064
```

Both tables in a teams match reached six clubs, and both tables received the unhelpful lead of the five of spades, the defence playing third highest leads from either a three card suit or an even number.

The Swedish declarer played three rounds of diamonds at once, then took a heart finesse before playing on clubs. When he found the 4-1 split he cashed the heart ace, ruffed another diamond, went back to the spade ace, and ruffed a third diamond. He still had the spade ace and the club ace to come, for twelve tricks.

At the other table Bjorn Fallenius introduced a diversion at trick one when he followed with the ten – which was either discouraging or an odd number. The French declarer took a trump finesse at once, then repeated it. When he found the 4-1 split he decided to assume the spade finesse was right, so he simply ran the spade jack, rather than take the heart finesse. The defence won and returned a spade. Declarer was left with insufficient entries to dummy to catch East's club honour by ruffing diamonds.

False Attitude

It is also sensible to lie about your attitude to discourage your partner's lead, when you can see that the obvious switch is the right defence.

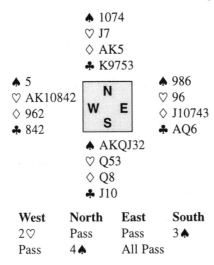

```
              ♠ 1074
              ♡ J7
              ◇ AK5
              ♣ K9753
♠ 5                         ♠ 986
♡ AK10842     N             ♡ 96
◇ 962       W   E           ◇ J10743
♣ 842         S             ♣ AQ6
              ♠ AKQJ32
              ♡ Q53
              ◇ Q8
              ♣ J10
```

West	North	East	South
2♡	Pass	Pass	3♠
Pass	4♠	All Pass	

When West leads the heart king you can see that if you show two hearts your partner will lead three rounds of the suit, letting the contract make. Discourage hearts and with any luck partner will find the club switch.

A variation on the same theme comes when you do like partner's lead – but can see that there are better defences for him than continuing the suit.

Love All. Teams.

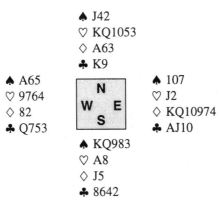

```
              ♠ J42
              ♡ KQ1053
              ◇ A63
              ♣ K9
♠ A65                       ♠ 107
♡ 9764        N             ♡ J2
◇ 82        W   E           ◇ KQ10974
♣ Q753        S             ♣ AJ10
              ♠ KQ983
              ♡ A8
              ◇ J5
              ♣ 8642
```

West	North	East	South
–	–	–	Pass
Pass	1♡	2◊	2♠
Pass	4♠	All Pass	

North's aggressive action, facing a passed hand partner, sets you a problem on defence. On the lead of the diamond eight declarer plays dummy's ace, and you can see that you need partner to get the lead via one of the majors, and shift to a club. If your partner shifts to a high club (denying an honour), then you will need to play him for a singleton diamond. If he shifts to a low club you will play your jack, hoping to get two club tricks and one diamond. So discourage at trick one by playing a low diamond, and hope partner does the right thing.

Another position where not enough thought is given to deception is when a side-suit is divided in such a way that at trick one you know that either your partner or declarer is void.

North/South Game. Teams.

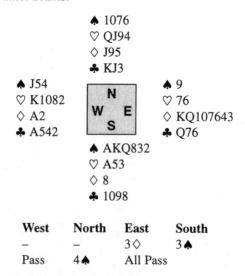

```
              ♠ 1076
              ♡ QJ94
              ◊ J95
              ♣ KJ3
♠ J54                       ♠ 9
♡ K1082      N              ♡ 76
◊ A2      W     E           ◊ KQ107643
♣ A542       S              ♣ Q76
              ♠ AKQ832
              ♡ A53
              ◊ 8
              ♣ 1098
```

West	North	East	South
–	–	3◊	3♠
Pass	4♠	All Pass	

On the lead of the diamond ace it is all too easy to fall into the trap of encouraging the opening lead – but you should work out that either declarer will ruff the next trick, or your encouragement will not mean much to a partner who began with a singleton. Dummy's hearts suggest that you might need to play clubs sooner rather than later – so it must be better to discourage the opening lead and hope for a club switch. (As a minor technical issue, if you wanted a heart switch, the diamond queen would shout for the higher suit here.)

False Suit-Preference

One of the things that becomes more apparent the longer you play the game is that the thing which divides the card players from the card pushers is the belief that every card means something. This means that in defence you can not afford to relax that much; it makes bridge harder, but a lot more enjoyable. Consequently, you will find that many players use an initial signal to be count or attitude, and a lot of subsequent signals to be suit preference. Let us then look at the distribution of a typical suit.

92

QJ73   AK1085

64

When West leads this (bid and supported) suit at trick one then East has a chance to signal count at trick one – his attitude is implicit because his side is just about to have won the trick. If West leads the jack at trick two then the size of East's card will carry a suit preference overtone.

Of course the danger with sending a message to your allies is that the enemy are standing by to intercept your words, to use them to their best advantage. In the second world war the Americans sent some of their messages in Navajo, as there was no-one on the Axis side who could interpret this language. Unfortunately the powers that be have banned the Bridge equivalent – encrypted signals – that is to say signals that are only interpretable by the sending side, so every signal carries some form of Government Health warning that it may damage your side as well as help it.

Of course it is frequently the case that getting the message to partner is the priority, and it does not matter that the enemy understand ... but that is not always the case. Let us look at two parallel examples, where the thinking bridge player will be able to work out that deception is necessary in one case, but potentially irrelevant or even harmful in the next.

(a)

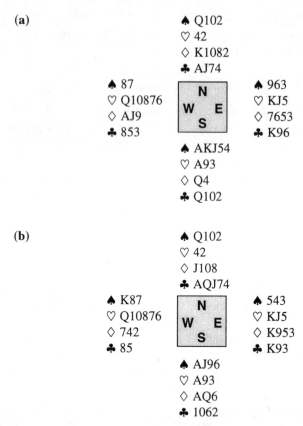

(b)

In both examples, South opens a strong no trump and is raised to game, and you lead the heart seven to your partner's king, ducked by declarer. When East returns the jack you can safely overtake, to drive out the ace.

In (a), you can see from your own high cards that there is a danger that declarer may succeed if partner wins his trick in a black suit, and switches to the other black suit. You can try to persuade your partner not to fall into that trap by showing an entry in the middle suit. Play the heart eight at trick three, which partner should be able to read as suit preference for the middle suit.

Example (b) is more difficult, but it looks as if declarer may have to guess whether to play on diamonds or spades for his nine tricks. If you are playing against someone who would not recognise a suit-preference signal if it bit him on the nose, then take the heart queen and return the ten as a suit preference signal for spades.

But if you are playing against someone who you respect, I would suggest playing a low heart at trick three. Now it is up to partner to make a good play; when he wins the second round of clubs (it looks routine to duck the first club in case declarer has only two) he should return the diamond nine, in itself a good deceptive play. He knows that if you had the spade ace, a sure immediate entry, you would probably have given true suit-preference; so you either have the diamond ace or the spade king; in either case, the diamond nine is the right card to play. If declarer still plays on diamonds not spades, you should be perversely pleased at the compliment he has paid your partnership.

There are many opportunities for deceptive suit preference based on the order in which you play your long suit; this was yet another example from the Minneapolis Nationals in 1994.

Love All. Teams.

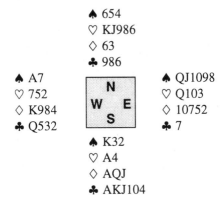

```
                  ♠ 654
                  ♡ KJ986
                  ◇ 63
                  ♣ 986
   ♠ A7          ┌─────────┐    ♠ QJ1098
   ♡ 752         │    N    │    ♡ Q103
   ◇ K984        │  W   E  │    ◇ 10752
   ♣ Q532        │    S    │    ♣ 7
                 └─────────┘
                  ♠ K32
                  ♡ A4
                  ◇ AQJ
                  ♣ AKJ104
```

South reached 3NT after East had pre-empted to show a bad hand with five or six spades. The defence led ace and a second spade, and JoAnn Manfield took the opportunity to signal on the second round of spades with the eight, her lowest spade, to indicate an entry in the lowest suit. Once declarer (who clearly belonged to the chauvinistic group who believe women are genetically incapable of deceiving men at the bridge table) had swallowed the bait, he was dead.

Perhaps it would have been more cautious to play a heart to the king for a club finesse, but he simply played the heart ace and took the heart finesse at once to go two down. Of course, if East had shown a heart entry at trick two declarer can succeed by playing on the minor suits, rather than by playing on hearts.

3
DECEPTION IN FOLLOWING SUIT

We have focused in the previous chapter on how there may be positions in which our signals – ostensibly aimed at our partner – may be distorted, for one of two purposes, namely either to deceive our partner or to deceive declarer. There are however many more positions where our deception arises from the card with which we follow suit.

Here the card is not a signal *per se* (which to my mind at least implies a degree of choice in the card played), but rather we want generally to convey the impression that our card is forced – that is to say that we did not have a choice as to the card we played.

This section is perhaps the most voluminous, and significant, of the areas in which deception may operate. Moreover, at least in part there are many single-suit combinations which recur with some frequency. If you can master and remember the ways to confuse declarer, and give him a losing option where none previously existed, then you are some way on the road to becoming a tough opponent.

There is no simple way, as declarer, to overcome the deceptions outlined here. My strategy as declarer is a relatively straightforward one; when an opponent makes a play which I can see is potentially a false card, I try to work out whether in a similar position I would have been able to find the same deception. If I would not have managed it, I assume the card to be genuine. You might look at it this way; if the player in question has found a play you would not have considered, then:

(a) He is probably a better player than you and would beat you in the long run anyway.

(b) Maybe the play deserves to succeed.

(c) The price of knowledge has never been cheap.

The Mandatory False Cards

Giving Declarer a Losing Option

Of all the sections in this book, this one is probably the most important; that is because I guarantee that you will be able to find an opportunity to put some of these plays into practice, sooner rather than later. Part of the problem with deception is that it is difficult to spot the tricky plays without having read them somewhere first. I am only scratching the surface here I know, but I hope that I have picked up on some of the most frequently occurring positions.

For our first section, put yourself in declarer's position in the South seat. How would you tackle these suits?

```
        AJ82                        AK82
K5       □□       1093      Q5       □□       1093
        Q764                        J764
```

Your natural play is to finesse the jack and lay down the ace in the first example, and to play off the ace and king in the second case. But, if East drops a nine or ten at his first opportunity, then you have to weigh up the chances of his holding the ten-nine doubleton – in which case your winning line is to cross back to hand and lead the honour from hand on the second round – which fails here of course.

The general point is obvious; where you have a pair of touching intermediates, be alive to the possibility of sacrificing one of them. However our next pair of cases have a similar, but slightly variant theme, involving declarer trying to establish a suit at no trumps.

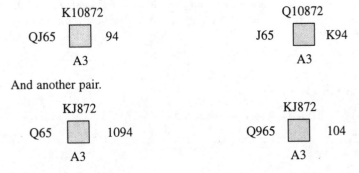

```
        K10872                      Q10872
QJ65     □□       94        J65      □□       K94
         A3                          A3
```

And another pair.

```
        KJ872                       KJ872
Q65      □□       1094      Q965     □□       104
         A3                          A3
```

In the first case the only 4-2 split you can cope with for one loser is to find the doubleton nine on your right, so in abstract your intention would be to lead ace and a small one to the ten. But, if East drops the nine on the first round, you have to contend with queen-nine or jack-nine doubleton, when the correct play would be to cash the king at the second trick. (We shall revisit this suit later.)

In the second case you appear to have a straight guess as to whether to play to the queen or the ten on the second round, but when the nine appears you may play East for the jack-nine doubleton and try the queen. (What's that? East might drop the jack from jack-nine doubleton? We'll come to that later too.) In the second pair of examples might the fall of the nine or ten distract you from finessing the jack? It shouldn't – but it might.

Some more examples of trying to persuade declarer to drop something that is not falling, come when declarer has a singleton trump in dummy.

	4				4	
J103		A5		963		AJ5
	KQ98762				KQ10872	

In the first example, when declarer leads the four to his queen your best shot at getting two trump tricks is to contribute the ten or jack to persuade declarer to try to pin your jack-ten doubleton. In the second case, declarer would undoubtedly play a trump to the ten if you let him alone. But contribute the jack on the first round to tempt him into playing you for ace-jack doubleton. Of course, the need for this last play only arises when you need two tricks specifically from this suit. If you might need three tricks you would duck, in case declarer has Q109xxx. But the play is quite safe from AJ9.

More singletons in dummy.

	5				5	
K4		J103		AJ6		Q9
	AQ98762				K1087432	

In the first example, suppose West is marked with the king, so South lays down the ace; East must falsecard by dropping the ten or jack to create the required ambiguity. In the second case West has opened the bidding, so you know declarer is going to play him for the ace. Following with the queen gives declarer two losing options – of playing your partner for A6, or you for QJ.

Of course then you have a problem in this last example of what to do with Q93 or J93. I think it is best to follow with the nine at your first turn – and hope declarer plays you for a doubleton honour.

In the first example, playing the king when the five is led from dummy gives declarer the chance to misguess on the second round. In the second case you need to give declarer an alternative to playing for the doubleton ace-king so West should play the jack at his first turn.

One final group – very similar in nature.

Clearly declarer has a chance to hold his losers to two, but if as East you follow with the nine or ten at your first turn you might nudge him in the wrong direction.

The cousins to these two are perhaps easier to spot; the falsecard is perhaps the natural instinctive play in any event – it just happens to create a losing option for declarer.

When declarer makes his initial play from dummy if you fail to play the nine or ten it leaves declarer no option but to try to drop the outstanding honour on the second round.

Sometimes you can generate remarkable results from very small cards, when declarer tries to read too much into them – though one should beware of trusting one's opponents too far in international matches.

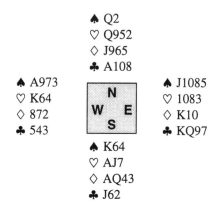

♠ Q2
♡ Q952
◇ J965
♣ A108

♠ A973
♡ K64
◇ 872
♣ 543

♠ J1085
♡ 1083
◇ K10
♣ KQ97

♠ K64
♡ AJ7
◇ AQ43
♣ J62

It looks normal, if slightly aggressive, to play in three no trumps, as indeed happened at both tables in the match between the Netherlands and Poland. Both Wests led a spade, won in dummy by the queen. The Dutch declarer made nine tricks in some comfort by taking an immediate diamond finesse and then laying down the ace of diamonds, dropping the king.

The Polish declarer took a slightly odd view when he led the diamond jack from dummy at trick two, to the king, ace and seven.

Now declarer took this card at face value – in which case his only chance would be the doubleton eight-seven of diamonds. He led the ace and jack of hearts from hand, with the West defender Wubbo de Boer ducking like a man who did not want to give him an entry to dummy for a diamond play. Eventually declarer got to dummy with the club ace to play the diamond nine, in an attempt to squash the eight – but the only thing that got squashed was his ego.

Another frequently occurring combination comes when declarer has to tackle:

AJ954

Q106   ☐   K8(2)

73(2)

Wherever the two in this suit is located, declarer figures to make the percentage play of a low card to the nine, intending to finesse the jack on the next round. But if West contributes an honour on the first round, declarer may be tempted to win the ace and play West for KQx.

(Of course the follow-up to that is that West should duck smoothly with KQx, expecting declarer to misguess; but maybe South will pay West the compliment of assuming he would play an honour from K10x ...?)

However the position does not have to be quite as straightforward as that; sometimes there are entry considerations to take account of as well. Look at this hand from a major pairs tournament in the USA.

Game All. Pairs.

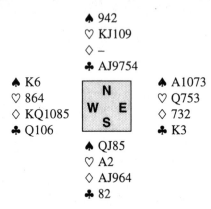

```
              ♠ 942
              ♡ KJ109
              ◇ –
              ♣ AJ9754
♠ K6           N          ♠ A1073
♡ 864       W     E       ♡ Q753
◇ KQ1085       S          ◇ 732
♣ Q106                    ♣ K3
              ♠ QJ85
              ♡ A2
              ◇ AJ964
              ♣ 82
```

It is not so easy for North-South to go plus on their cards – but one would certainly not think 3NT by South was necessarily where you wanted to finish.

Joanne Manfield and Danny Sprung were defending, and the opening lead of a heart was won by declarer in hand, to play a club towards dummy. Manfield hopped up with the queen, was allowed to hold the trick, and a second heart to East's queen for a diamond switch meant declarer had to get the clubs right by rising with the ace, to make the contract. When he misguessed, dummy was dead and the contract finished up four down.

Right, time for a new theme; this time our efforts are going to be directed to persuading declarer that we have shortage when in fact we have length, so that he generates an extra loser.

Three pairs of linked hands here; first, the duck.

```
      AJ5                        KJ52
  4  [   ]  K1083            4  [   ]  A1083
      Q9762                       Q976
```

In both instances you are trying to deflect declarer from the winning line, of leading low to the jack, and then playing dummy's top card. In both cases you may succeed by dropping your eight on the first round. If you do, declarer may try to pin the ten-eight in the first instance by leading the queen from hand; and, in the second example, he may lead low back to the queen at the second trick.

Next pair; the falsecard on a losing trick.

In the first case, declarer will play the king followed by the ace unless you drop the nine, and get him to start worrying about that being a singleton. (Declarer may avoid this problem by tackling the suit by leading initially from dummy – then East cannot falsecard in total safety as West might have the singleton ten.) In the second example, declarer will surely play the ace and king – unless your eight persuades him to try and pin the ten-eight by crossing to hand to lead the jack.

And finally in this section, the falsecard on the winning trick.

It is fairly clear that declarer will lose the first trick in these suits to your partner's singleton honour. To give him a chance to go wrong on the next round, drop the eight like a man with a singleton and hope declarer is watching your cards!

If we can do all of that with small cards, imagine how much fun we can have with honours that we do not need.

Well, to start with we can try to tempt declarer into an indiscreet finesse.

AK1072   AK9732
Q5 [ ] J4   86 [ ] J104
9863   Q5

It does no harm to 'split your honours' in the first case when declarer leads low from hand – who knows, it may tempt declarer into the 'idiot's finesse', by crossing back to hand to lead to dummy's ten? In the second case the odds may technically favour taking a finesse if a high card appears – but if you have any respect for East as a player, ignore this falsecard.

Playing the Honour from Honour-ten Doubleton

There are many positions where this is a possible play. Sometimes it is simply to create a losing option when declarer has a choice of cards to crash:

	4				42	
Q76		K10		Q76		K10
	AJ98532				AJ9853	

(No further entries to dummy)

In both these instances when declarer leads from dummy playing the king at your first turn would allow declarer to try to drop king-queen doubleton unsuccessfully. The same play works from queen-ten doubleton – but beware: if declarer has an eight card suit you may be clearing up a guess for him.

Sometimes dropping an honour allows declarer to finesse on the way back, under the assumption that you have a singleton.

	J92				J92	
743		K10		743		Q10
	AQ865				AK865	

Dropping the honour as East may persuade declarer to play low to the nine on the second round. Mind you, you have to be reasonably confident that declarer has both the missing two top honours – otherwise the play risks throwing a trick – but, even so, declarer may still finesse into your ten.

More of the same, when declarer has a 6-2 fit and you have queen-ten.

	AKJ942				KJ9432	
865		Q10		865		Q10
	73				A7	

Perhaps declarer was going to finesse on the second round anyway, but you give him a different problem if you drop the queen on the first round. Don't drop the queen if declarer has a 5-3 fit; you give him a chance to play off a second honour to test if the suit is 4-1 and only then to finesse, with say KJ943 facing A72.

The lowly ten-eight doubleton has its part to play as well, in a little known falsecard. I first saw this in the European Championships in 1989 – and I have been waiting since then for its reappearance!

972

AK5   ▢   108

QJ643

Declarer simply led up to the queen-jack twice and held his losers to two. But if East had played the ten on the first round, might declarer have played low to the seven on the second round?

There are a couple of related themes where fooling around from Honour – ten-eight can bring unexpected rewards. These plays are pretty safe when dummy has the nine, although they sometimes give the optical illusion of wasting a card you cannot afford.

North/South Game. Teams.

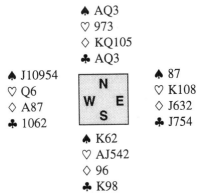

♠ AQ3
♡ 973
◇ KQ105
♣ AQ3

♠ J10954
♡ Q6
◇ A87
♣ 1062

♠ 87
♡ K108
◇ J632
♣ J754

♠ K62
♡ AJ542
◇ 96
♣ K98

When South opens the bidding with one heart it excites North to some show of action before he subsides in four hearts. Your partner leads a stolid jack of spades, and you can see that some fireworks may be necessary to beat this contract. Declarer wins the ace as you follow with the eight, then plays a heart to the ten, jack and queen. Your partner plays a second spade, and when declarer wins this in hand he has a real problem. If you have the bare heart ten he cannot afford to lay down the heart ace now, or he will lose three trump tricks and the diamond ace. If he takes your card as honest he may lead a low heart from hand. You win your king, and lead a diamond to your partner's ace, and get a spade ruff for the setting trick.

And now for the acknowledged master holding when it comes to falsecards – there are probably at least twice as many good falsecards involving jack-nine combinations as I will quote here, almost all of them risk-free, which is always a bonus!

Imagine you are declarer as South, with the lead in dummy.

```
        10853                           1085
  K  [      ]  AJ9            32  [      ]  AJ9
        Q7642                          KQ764
```

Left to your own devices you would surely hold your losers to two in this suit in the first instance by leading low from dummy, and ducking when the nine appears (this is correct when West has a singleton ace or king, and wrong when East has ducked smoothly from AK9). But if East contributes the jack ...? And similarly in the second instance you will play up to the king-queen twice, and not think any more about it, unless East drops the jack on the first round, when you may finesse the eight on the second round.

(In some cases East can afford the jack from the bare jack-nine, i.e. in positions such as the second example, if he knows his side need two tricks from the suit to beat the contract.)

This last position brings us on to two comparable situations.

```
     (lead in dummy)                (lead in hand)
        10853                          K1085
 642 [      ] AJ9           AJ9 [      ] 642
         KQ7                            Q73
```

Declarer will surely play these two suits for one loser if left to his own devices, but you have paid your entry fee and are entitled to contribute the jack on the first round. In the first case declarer may take a finesse of the ten-eight on the third round, and with the second holding declarer may finesse the seven on the second round.

Do you remember we were looking at this combination earlier?

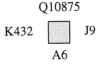

Q10875

K432   J9

A6

We have changed the defensive layout now; won't declarer lead to the eight on the second round if you drop the jack from this holding – or even perhaps from J93?

Again, the sight of a full hand may make the position clearer. Again the provenance is a US tournament.

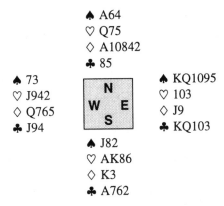

♠ A64
♡ Q75
◇ A10842
♣ 85

♠ 73   ♠ KQ1095
♡ J942   ♡ 103
◇ Q765   ◇ J9
♣ J94   ♣ KQ103

♠ J82
♡ AK86
◇ K3
♣ A762

West had a tough lead after a strong no trump was raised to three, and his selection of a fourth highest heart did not unduly discomfit declarer, who won in hand, and laid down the diamond king. When Lou Reich contributed the jack, it looked safe to declarer to play a diamond to the eight next. After all, if it lost it would presumably be to the queen. Alas for him, the defence could now get two diamond tricks, and declarer had only eight tricks.

If Reich had followed with the nine at his first turn might declarer still have gone wrong, playing him for a tricky 9x holding? Perhaps, but the a posteriori reasoning must be that, if he did not play him to have falsecarded with one holding, he would not play him to have falsecarded from another!

There are many situations where the trump holding of jack-nine generates some action by some unusual play. For example Benito Garozzo, the Italian world champion, defeated a slam where the trump layout was as follows:

8765

J9   [   ]   K3

AQ1042

When the nine was led at trick one, even when the opening leader was Garozzo, declarer thought it was right to take two finesses. Note that, if declarer has this nine card holding and tackles it himself by leading low to the queen, you can drop the jack with no risk. Perhaps he will now cross to dummy to repeat the finesse, in a suit you can ruff.

To close up this section, let me give you a couple of hands defended by two master players. First Martin Hoffman, perhaps the best card-player never to have made it to the Great Britain team. After West opened one diamond South became declarer in four hearts. Our hero was in the East seat.

Game All. Pairs.

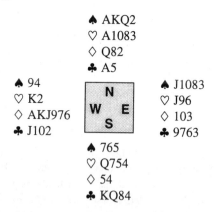

♠ AKQ2
♥ A1083
♦ Q82
♣ A5

♠ 94   ♠ J1083
♥ K2   ♥ J96
♦ AKJ976   ♦ 103
♣ J102   ♣ 9763

♠ 765
♥ Q754
♦ 54
♣ KQ84

West led two rounds of diamonds, and switched to the club jack. South won in dummy and tried to tempt Hoffman into shortening his trumps, by leading a third round of diamonds, but Hoffman discarded a club. Now declarer led the ace of hearts and a second heart; Hoffman contributed the jack on the second round, and declarer naturally played the queen. West could win the king and play a fourth round of diamonds, repromoting Hoffman's heart nine!

The final example comes from the Sunday Times of 1990, regarded as the strongest invitation event in the World. In the West seat was Bobby Goldman, who with his regular partner, Paul Soloway, has been one of the dominant pairs in US Bridge for 15 years.

Game All. Teams.

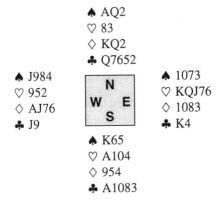

♠ AQ2
♡ 83
◇ KQ2
♣ Q7652

♠ J984
♡ 952
◇ AJ76
♣ J9

♠ 1073
♡ KQJ76
◇ 1083
♣ K4

♠ K65
♡ A104
◇ 954
♣ A1083

After East had overcalled one heart, North-South propelled themselves to
3NT and Goldman led a heart, which declarer, Christian Mari of France,
had to duck till the third round. Now it was essential to keep East off lead
or he would cash his heart winners, so Mari played a spade to table and
called for the club queen, which went king, ace, jack! Not unreasonably,
Mari thought that he could cross to table again with a spade for the finesse
of the club nine. However, Goldman won, and played a third spade. Now
he had a spade winner to cash when he got in with the diamond ace for the
defence's fifth trick, a truly remarkable result.

Playing the Card You are Known to Hold

There are occasions when the play to date marks a defender with a certain
card. Very often, playing this card at the first opportunity can create doubt
in declarer's mind. This theme emerges frequently when declarer has taken
a winning finesse, thus implicitly marking a card in one defender's hand.

AJ4

Q102   876

K953

Declarer tackles the suit by taking the finesse of the jack. When it holds,
you are marked with the queen; so play it under the ace. Now declarer has
to decide whether to finesse on the next round or not. If you follow with
the ten, he has no guess because he knows you have the queen. Once you
have seen it, it becomes obvious – now try the next suit.

```
              K862
      A75      [ ]      J94
              Q103
```

Declarer leads the two to his ten and the ace. You must drop the jack under the queen on the next round to give declarer a problem.

Sometimes it is not a question of an actual trick in the suit in question, rather of preventing declarer from getting a cross-ruff going efficiently. Let us look at this side-suit in a trump contract.

```
              94
      J72      [ ]      K105
              AQ863
```

When declarer takes the finesse and then lays down the ace, then unless there is no further entry to dummy you know that your partner has the jack, or declarer would have repeated the finesse. So drop the king on the second round to leave declarer guessing whether to ruff the third round high or low.

We saw earlier that there were some shenanigans available to the defence with a holding of honour-ten-eight. This elegant example combines some of those themes with the point about playing the known card.

North/South Game. Teams.

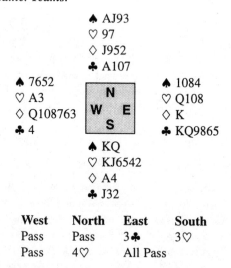

```
              ♠ AJ93
              ♡ 97
              ◊ J952
              ♣ A107
♠ 7652                        ♠ 1084
♡ A3          N               ♡ Q108
◊ Q108763   W   E             ◊ K
♣ 4           S               ♣ KQ9865
              ♠ KQ
              ♡ KJ6542
              ◊ A4
              ♣ J32
```

West	North	East	South
Pass	Pass	3♣	3♡
Pass	4♡	All Pass	

Game All. Teams.

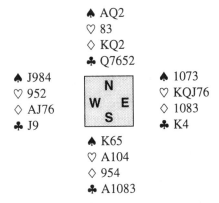

```
              ♠ AQ2
              ♡ 83
              ◇ KQ2
              ♣ Q7652
  ♠ J984              ♠ 1073
  ♡ 952       N       ♡ KQJ76
  ◇ AJ76    W   E     ◇ 1083
  ♣ J9        S       ♣ K4
              ♠ K65
              ♡ A104
              ◇ 954
              ♣ A1083
```

After East had overcalled one heart, North-South propelled themselves to 3NT and Goldman led a heart, which declarer, Christian Mari of France, had to duck till the third round. Now it was essential to keep East off lead or he would cash his heart winners, so Mari played a spade to table and called for the club queen, which went king, ace, jack! Not unreasonably, Mari thought that he could cross to table again with a spade for the finesse of the club nine. However, Goldman won, and played a third spade. Now he had a spade winner to cash when he got in with the diamond ace for the defence's fifth trick, a truly remarkable result.

Playing the Card You are Known to Hold

There are occasions when the play to date marks a defender with a certain card. Very often, playing this card at the first opportunity can create doubt in declarer's mind. This theme emerges frequently when declarer has taken a winning finesse, thus implicitly marking a card in one defender's hand.

```
              AJ4
      Q102    [  ]    876
              K953
```

Declarer tackles the suit by taking the finesse of the jack. When it holds, you are marked with the queen; so play it under the ace. Now declarer has to decide whether to finesse on the next round or not. If you follow with the ten, he has no guess because he knows you have the queen. Once you have seen it, it becomes obvious – now try the next suit.

```
                K862
        A75   [    ]   J94
                Q103
```

Declarer leads the two to his ten and the ace. You must drop the jack under the queen on the next round to give declarer a problem.

Sometimes it is not a question of an actual trick in the suit in question, rather of preventing declarer from getting a cross-ruff going efficiently. Let us look at this side-suit in a trump contract.

```
                 94
        J72   [     ]   K105
               AQ863
```

When declarer takes the finesse and then lays down the ace, then unless there is no further entry to dummy you know that your partner has the jack, or declarer would have repeated the finesse. So drop the king on the second round to leave declarer guessing whether to ruff the third round high or low.

We saw earlier that there were some shenanigans available to the defence with a holding of honour-ten-eight. This elegant example combines some of those themes with the point about playing the known card.

North/South Game. Teams.

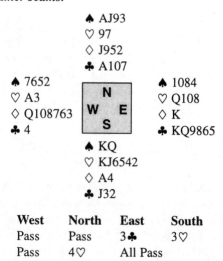

```
                ♠ AJ93
                ♡ 97
                ◇ J952
                ♣ A107
♠ 7652                        ♠ 1084
♡ A3          N              ♡ Q108
◇ Q108763   W   E            ◇ K
♣ 4            S             ♣ KQ9865
                ♠ KQ
                ♡ KJ6542
                ◇ A4
                ♣ J32
```

West	North	East	South
Pass	Pass	3♣	3♡
Pass	4♡	All Pass	

When your partner leads his club declarer can see that he has his work cut out for him. If he wins the ace and plays on spades he has little chance – so the best hope must be to find you with queen and another heart. He plays a heart to the jack (on which you contribute the ten) and your partner wins his ace, and optimistically switches to a diamond, to the nine, king and ace. Declarer lays down the heart king, on which you contribute the known card, the queen, and comes to the cross-roads.

If he thinks you have the eight of hearts left – in which case he must be a very untrusting soul – he can succeed by playing off the top spades, overtaking the queen. The convenient fall of the ten allows him two discards for his losing clubs, but it fails when your partner is 5-3-4-1. As against that, if he believes you have two hearts, he simply plays a diamond towards dummy, to establish another sure discard for his club loser; this line fails of course, when you ruff your partner's winner (to avoid accidents) and cash your two club tricks.

There is a series of slightly less regularly occurring positions where an initial finesse has succeeded, and you need to preserve some ambiguity.

	KJ72				KJ752	
AQ96		1054		AQ96		104
	83				83	

In the first example, where this is a side-suit in a trump contract, declarer leads to the king and exits with a low card; win the ace, the card you are known to hold, and declarer has no certainty that he can subsequently ruff the suit back to hand without fear of an over-ruff. In the second example, in no trumps, declarer leads low to the jack, and then comes back to hand to lead low again. Play the queen; this way declarer does not know the suit is 4-2. If you play the nine declarer will score his king and may then switch his attack because he knows the suit is not behaving.

A couple of more complex examples; in the first dummy has no outside entries.

	AQ1074	
KJ96		8
	532	

Declarer leads low to the ten and then comes back to hand to lead up to dummy again. Play the jack and declarer will cover with the queen – getting only three tricks from the suit. If you duck, then declarer can work out that the suit is 4-1. He ducks too, and later repeats the finesse to make four tricks.

On the following hand the defence have to find a good play, and West may find it more difficult than normal because the sight of dummy may depress his hopes of getting two tricks.

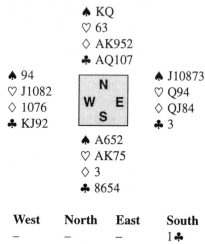

```
                    ♠ KQ
                    ♡ 63
                    ◊ AK952
                    ♣ AQ107
  ♠ 94                           ♠ J10873
  ♡ J1082          N             ♡ Q94
  ◊ 1076        W     E          ◊ QJ84
  ♣ KJ92           S             ♣ 3
                    ♠ A652
                    ♡ AK75
                    ◊ 3
                    ♣ 8654
```

West	North	East	South
–	–	–	1♣
Pass	2◊	Pass	2♡
Pass	3♣	Pass	3NT
Pass	6♣	All Pass	

You lead the heart jack with high expectations of your trump suit, and are bitterly disappointed by the dummy. Declarer wins the ace of hearts and plays a club to the ten, on which your partner plays the three. Now declarer comes to the heart king and plays a spade to hand. When he plays a second club it is essential to follow with the jack. Why? Well you know what the trump position is but declarer has to consider that East might have K93, in which case taking a second finesse would allow East to play a third trump – which could be fatal. If trumps are 3-2 declarer can rise with the club ace and cross-ruff in comfort to twelve tricks.

If declarer plays the club ace, the best he can do thereafter is to cash dummy's top spades, play ace king of diamonds and ruff a diamond, and lead the spade ace in this ending:

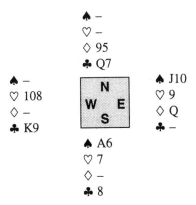

If you ruff low, declarer can still succeed, but you can throw a heart away (or ruff high and exit with a trump) and declarer must fail. Again, playing the club jack, the card you were inferentially known to hold, was critical.

Sometimes the card you are known to hold is not an honour – this is however the only example I have seen where the significant card is as low as an eight.

Love All. Teams.

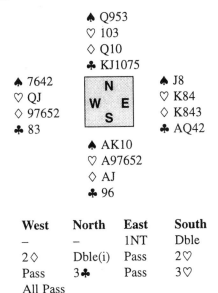

West	North	East	South
–	–	1NT	Dble
2◊	Dble(i)	Pass	2♡
Pass	3♣	Pass	3♡
All Pass			

(i) Values

Against three hearts, your partner leads the club eight, and you obediently play three rounds of that suit; declarer ruffs the third round with the six, overruffed with the jack. Now partner plays the diamond seven (marking him with five low diamonds) to dummy's ten.

At this point you need to do two good things to have a chance to beat the contract. First duck the diamond, to deny declarer an extra entry to dummy.

Secondly, when declarer crosses to table with the spade queen to lead a low heart, play the eight – remember, you are marked with this card; partner would have over-ruffed with it if he had it. Now declarer has to decide whether to play the nine or the ace; one is right if you began life with K84, the other if you began with KQ8 – not so easy. If you had followed with the four then, as you are marked with the eight, declarer's only hope is that you began with K84 or Q84, as he cannot cope with KQ84.

(Yes, declarer might succeed if he makes his first trump play from hand – but nobody is perfect!)

Playing the Top of a Sequence of Honours

This is another section with a lot of meat in it; what we are looking at is a conscious decision to follow with a deceptively high card, and the purpose is to mislead any or all three of the other people at the table – though dummy is a lower priority than declarer, it must be admitted.

Let us look at the opening trick, where we are intending to deceive both partner and declarer – for the most part. Before we get on to deception let us look at a little-known defensive signal, which might come in useful one day for you.

873

Q65   ⬚   AKJ94

102

Partner finds a good lead in an unbid suit against 3NT, and you have to decide how to get him to unblock the queen; if you lead low at trick two declarer may turn up with an embarrassing queen-two! The answer is to win trick one with the ace, and then play the king – this being a request for an unblock.

Of course, another technical reason for playing ace then king is to show a doubleton; and a third possibility is that you may also have a suit-preference message to pass on.

But leaving aside the technical reasons for winning with the ace rather than the king, there is a very common reason for making this play – which tends to be rather under-used. The aim is to mislead declarer about the location of the high cards – if you win the king you tend to pinpoint the remaining high cards in your partner's hand. Let us look at an example to see how such a slight false card can have a big effect.

East/West Game. Teams.

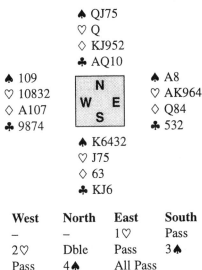

```
                    ♠ QJ75
                    ♡ Q
                    ◇ KJ952
                    ♣ AQ10
      ♠ 109                        ♠ A8
      ♡ 10832        N             ♡ AK964
      ◇ A107      W     E          ◇ Q84
      ♣ 9874         S             ♣ 532
                    ♠ K6432
                    ♡ J75
                    ◇ 63
                    ♣ KJ6
```

West	North	East	South
–	–	1♡	Pass
2♡	Dble	Pass	3♠
Pass	4♠	All Pass	

West leads the heart two and you can see that the only issue on the hand will be the diamond guess. If you win the heart king at trick one, South will discover you have the spade ace before negotiating diamonds – at which point it would be logical to assume West must have the diamond ace for him to have dredged up the initial response. But if you win the heart ace at trick one and play a club, the reverse logic will apply. South will not be able to construct an opening bid for you without the diamond ace, and he will surely therefore go wrong in diamonds.

An alternative reason for the ace-king falsecard is that you can set up a ruffing finesse position for declarer. If a side-suit is divided along the following lines:

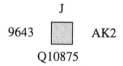

If you take your king when your partner leads this suit, declarer will have the successful option of ruffing out your ace-king, but if you win the first trick with the ace you give him the losing option of the ruffing finesse.

Why else should you win the first trick with the ace from ace-king? Well maybe the suit is set out like this:

```
        983                              983
J752    ▓    AK4              J765       ▓    AK4
        Q106                             Q102
```

our aim if we need three quick tricks from the suit is to win the ace and return a low card to put declarer to the guess. This is a suit combination which may lead to deceptive play by both declarer and the defence. Declarer in the second example could discourage us from trying this manoeuvre by concealing the two – so we do not know if our partner has led from a five card suit – but he can do nothing deceptive in the first case. We know that partner has a four card suit when he leads the two, so the underlead at trick two should (errors and omissions excepting) be safe.

One of the most under used falsecards comes when partner leads a suit in which you have a pair of touching honours. It is normal practice to follow with the lower of the honours, which is helpful to both declarer and partner. Let us look at some suit layouts where the fact that partner is misled may be secondary to fooling declarer (though, having said that, it would be helpful for partner to know our tendencies here).

Let us look first at the king-queen.

```
        AJ72                             AJ72
10864   ▓    KQ5              9764       ▓    KQ5
        93                               103
```

If we win the queen at the first opportunity declarer may work out that we have KQx, and ruff out our other honour, but we certainly make life more difficult for him by playing the king initially. In the second case declarer may be lured into finessing twice if we win the first trick with the king.

Sometimes the effect of winning with the king from king-queen will be to
discourage partner from continuing the suit. If this is the lay-out at no trumps:

4

J752   KQ3

A10986

When partner leads the two, you know that declarer has a five card suit. It
may be worth considering playing the king at trick one to discourage
partner from setting up declarer's suit.

What about the queen-jack?

(a)

AK104

8652   QJ7

93

(b)

K1084

A652   QJ7

93

It looks right in the first example to win the first trick with the queen to
lure declarer into a second finesse; just hope partner does not feel obliged
to discard all of his holding too soon. In the second case we want to
persuade declarer to get the second finesse wrong, and we boost our
chances by the falsecard.

Of course it should go without saying that it is vital, if you are to attempt
these deceptive plays, that your partner is tuned in to the possibility that
you could try a spot of skull-duggery. In the second example, your play
might lead partner to rise with the ace prematurely, on the second round of
the suit, if he believes declarer has the jack; so, if you are playing with a
relatively inexperienced partner, this sort of falsecard may not be worth
the effort.

Sometimes when partner has led from shortage you can disguise the fact
with the queen-jack falsecard. Say partner has led a singleton in a suit
contract, and you have the trump ace.

Real-life

984

3   QJ752

AK106

Pretending to be

984

J753   Q2

AK106

You play the queen at trick one, then win your ace of trumps and continue with the two. Declarer has a tough problem.

Certainly the jack-ten has many moments. For example, consider these positions at trick one.

(a) **(b)**

```
        Q973                        K973
K854  [    ]  J106        A854  [    ]  J106
        A2                          Q2
```

With both these jack-ten holdings the sight of dummy may persuade us to play the jack.

Sometimes we can try to protect our jack-ten holding from further embarrassment after an indiscreet lead, by making a falsecard.

```
           Q975
      3  [    ]  J1064
           AK82
```

When partner finds a bad moment to lead his singleton, declarer can easily pick up our holding for no loser. But maybe we can give South a nudge in the wrong direction by following with the jack at trick one, trying to persuade declarer that West has 10643. (Of course declarer may still go wrong if you play the ten. But if he is a creature of habit who starts his reasoning 'East can not have the jack-ten because ...' then the falsecard must be the right strategy.)

There are other cases at trick one where we would like to lull declarer into a false sense of security.

```
           J96
    542  [    ]  KQ107
           A83
```

When partner leads the four (second from a bad suit), play the queen, and declarer may not try to dispose of one of his losers via a successful finesse in a side-suit, he may simply expect that the ten is onside for him, losing two tricks in this suit in the fullness of time. Sometimes the position is a little akin to signalling discouragement, when a switch is appropriate.

Let's look at a full hand where we manipulate our honours to get partner to do the right thing.

Teams.

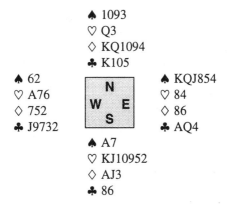

♠ 1093
♡ Q3
◇ KQ1094
♣ K105

♠ 62   ♠ KQJ854
♡ A76   ♡ 84
◇ 752   ◇ 86
♣ J9732   ♣ AQ4

♠ A7
♡ KJ10952
◇ AJ3
♣ 86

North-South brush your one spade opening aside to reach four hearts.

When partner leads the spade six you know that if he gets in again he may need to find the club switch to beat the contract. Make it easy for him by playing the spade king at trick one, to deny the queen. Now the club shift becomes trivial – maybe he should find it anyway but there is no harm in being kind to partner.

Playing Unnecessarily High

Let us have a look at some deceptive ways to win tricks on declarer's suits.

KJ1094

652   [ ]   AQ87

3

If declarer needs three tricks in this side suit to make his slam he will lead to the nine, and later on will take a ruffing finesse successfully. If we win the first trick with the ace we may persuade declarer to try to drop our partner's hypothetical Qxx, by ruffing out the suit. No dice.

Why else should we win the ace when we could win the queen? Maybe we are defending a slam in another suit.

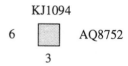

KJ1094

6   AQ8752

3

When partner leads the suit at trick one we may lull declarer into a false sense of security if we win the ace and return a low one. Declarer may discard, or ruff too low, whereas winning the queen might tip him off to the danger.

About fifteen years ago the English Bridge Union magazine published a hand from an unfeeling husband, comparing his wife to the Rueful Rabbit, who as you will recall occasionally gets things right without knowing why. This was the hand, as I recall it, which had driven him to put pen to paper.

Teams.

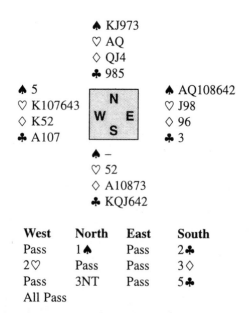

♠ KJ973
♡ AQ
◇ QJ4
♣ 985

♠ 5
♡ K107643
◇ K52
♣ A107

♠ AQ108642
♡ J98
◇ 96
♣ 3

♠ –
♡ 52
◇ A10873
♣ KQJ642

West	North	East	South
Pass	1♠	Pass	2♣
2♡	Pass	Pass	3◇
Pass	3NT	Pass	5♣
All Pass			

When our narrator led his singleton spade South, the victim of the piece, naturally contributed the jack from dummy. East, as if it were the most natural thing in the world, played the ace, and declarer ruffed. The queen of clubs won the next trick, then West took his club ace on the next round of trumps and played the heart seven. I ask you: does it not look natural to take the ace and play the spade king to discard your heart loser? Now, West can ruff, and still has the diamond king to come for one down.

Sometimes the object is to persuade declarer to waste his entries or simply pure sadism, to build up his hopes and then dash them.

```
              Q10875
   642      [      ]      AKJ
                93
```

Declarer, who is short of entries to hand, crosses to lead the nine in this suit. Win the king, so as to persuade declarer to make an unnecessary journey to repeat the finesse.

What about this trump suit?

```
               985
   AKJ      [      ]      74
              Q10632
```

You lead a side-suit and force declarer to ruff in hand, then, when declarer crosses to dummy to run the nine, you win the first trump with the king and force him again. Surely declarer will finesse in trumps again; now you draw trumps to run your suit; if you had won the first trick cheaply, declarer would have seen this coming and been more cautious.

If you can make this play with the AKJ, you can certainly do it with the AQx. Sometimes the right strategy with this holding (or even AQxx) in trumps is to hold up altogether, or to win the first trick with the ace, to mislead declarer or to lull him to sleep prematurely.

Let us see a full hand.

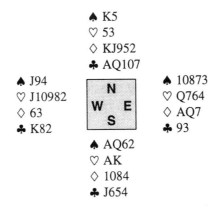

```
                    ♠ K5
                    ♡ 53
                    ◇ KJ952
                    ♣ AQ107
   ♠ J94                           ♠ 10873
   ♡ J10982         N              ♡ Q764
   ◇ 63         W       E          ◇ AQ7
   ♣ K82             S              ♣ 93
                    ♠ AQ62
                    ♡ AK
                    ◇ 1084
                    ♣ J654
```

It is not so easy to bid these hands to five clubs by North after a weak no trump from South; nonetheless when North-South come to rest in 3NT it seems as if declarer's normal line succeeds. As South you would win the heart lead, lose the diamond finesse to East, and fall back on the clubs, which do behave. But what if East wins the first diamond with the ace, not the queen? Surely, declarer simply repeats the diamond finesse confidently? Oops.

Another example in a suit declarer is developing, possibly even in the trump suit.

Q1043

5 [   ] KJ72

A986

If declarer tackles this suit by leading to the ten then you will certainly only score one trick if you win the jack, as declarer has a simple finesse against you. But if you win the king, will not declarer play your partner for a possible J752, and play to the ace on the next round?

It is usually easier, and more satisfying, to look at a full hand. In the 1990 World Team Championships in Geneva a variation of the king-jack position came up – nicely solved in defence by Ralph Katz.

Teams.

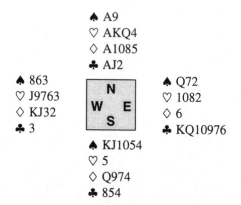

The Russian South reached six diamonds, East having shown clubs, and received a club lead. He won the ace to cash three rounds of hearts to discard his club losers, and then immediately played a diamond to the seven and king. When he ruffed the heart return he thought he knew the whole story. He would draw a second round of trumps with the ace, then play ace and king of spades, and run the jack of spades, East being 2-3-2-6.

Of course once he played a diamond to the ace he had a second loser in trumps; but if Katz had thoughtlessly won the first trump with the jack, declarer would have had no option but to finesse in diamonds, and subsequently, because of the entries, to play East successfully for the spade queen.

Try the same ploy with this variation on the same theme.

Q104

532   ⬜   KJ7

A986

What about this one, if truly desperate measures are called for?

Declarer is known to hold three cards only in the suit, and dummy is entryless.

A1098

762   ⬜   KJ4

Q53

Declarer plays low to the ten, and it is clear that you can hold declarer to two tricks by taking the jack now. But maybe you are prepared to have a little gamble to try to hold him to one trick.

Say you win the first trick with the king. Won't declarer play the queen on the second round, and finesse the nine on the next round? Even if declarer starts by running the queen you might try ducking! Then declarer will play small to the nine and your jack; and on the third round he will surely finesse again.

It is worth noting by the way that there are similar sorts of deceptive possibilities with an entryless dummy if you know declarer has three cards in this suit.

A1098

762   ⬜   Q53

KJ4

Declarer runs the jack and you duck, then he plays the king and repeats the finesse, you hope.

Sacrificing Honours

There are many reasons to sacrifice an honour; sometimes it is to give declarer a losing option, when he has to decide if your honour is a singleton or not.

AQ108432

KJ 95

76

Declarer plays this suit to an entryless dummy in no trumps, and will have no problems if you play the jack. But he will probably duck your king, if you play it, to ensure he can run the suit.

An unlikely one I know, but perhaps you can persuade declarer to take his eye off the ball and forget his safety plays with this entryless dummy;

AKJ7432

Q1098 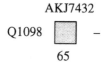 –

65

Declarer should duck the first round of this suit entirely to ensure he can take six tricks from this suit – but if you play the queen at your first opportunity he might have a rush of blood to the head.

Let us have a look at a full hand where the sacrifice of an honour in an unusual position could sneak under declarer's guard.

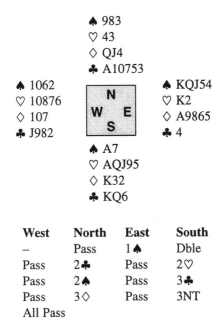

♠ 983
♡ 43
◇ QJ4
♣ A10753

♠ 1062   ♠ KQJ54
♡ 10876   ♡ K2
◇ 107   ◇ A9865
♣ J982   ♣ 4

♠ A7
♡ AQJ95
◇ K32
♣ KQ6

West	North	East	South
–	Pass	1♠	Dble
Pass	2♣	Pass	2♡
Pass	2♠	Pass	3♣
Pass	3◇	Pass	3NT
All Pass			

You lead a spade against 3NT, and get a complete count of declarer's hand at once – his delayed club support implies that he must be 2-5-3-3. Your partner leads two rounds of spades, and declarer wins the second spade, cashes the king and queen of clubs, intending to run the clubs and pressurise East, then take a heart finesse and see what happens.

Is there anything you can do to stop him?

If you drop the club jack on the second round, apparently, declarer has suddenly acquired an extra entry to table. If he overtakes the queen to take another heart finesse, all of a sudden, his five club tricks are down to three. Even the king of hearts coming down in two rounds does not give him enough top tricks, and East is poised to cash out for down one as soon as a diamond is played.

Another good reason for dropping an honour prematurely comes about when a suit is behaving very favourably for declarer, and you want to persuade him otherwise.

Sometimes it may be simply a question of persuading declarer to waste precious entries; we have seen already that you can sacrifice the jack in this position:

8765

J4 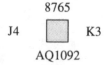 K3

AQ1092

when declarer finesses. All these honours can go under the knife as well ...

AKQ2   Q1065

J74  983   K74  J98

1065   A32

In the first example, sacrifice the jack on the second round, to persuade declarer to play the third round to the ten; perhaps he will have problems getting back to dummy.

In the second case, if declarer plays the ace and a second round, play the jack whether declarer guesses the suit or not.

More of the same.

AK1085   KJ93

Q6  J7   Q74  1082

9432   A65

If declarer is marked with four cards and lays down the ace in the first example you should follow with the jack, so that declarer has to cross to hand to take a finesse. In the second case declarer lays down the ace from hand and plays to the jack, allowing you to follow with the ten, and misrepresent the suit to declarer.

Sometimes the play is massive deception.

Q7432

KJ9 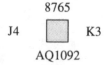 865

A10

When declarer sets about this suit at no trumps, dropping the king under the ace may persuade him that the suit is 5-1 and he should turn his attentions elsewhere.

Sometimes we are looking at something more subtle than that.

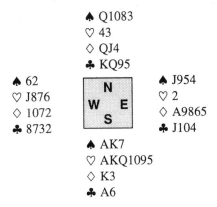

♠ Q1083
♡ 43
◇ QJ4
♣ KQ95

♠ 62   ♠ J954
♡ J876   ♡ 2
◇ 1072   ◇ A9865
♣ 8732   ♣ J104

♠ AK7
♡ AKQ1095
◇ K3
♣ A6

Your partner's opening lead ability lets him down against six hearts, as he leads a spade to declarer's ace, rather than a diamond. Declarer cashes the ace, king and queen of hearts, then follows with the spade king. If you play a low spade, declarer (who now needs West to follow to at least three clubs) should next cash the three top clubs. With the highly favourable developments in that suit, declarer can next play the club nine, to discard his last diamond.

But if you drop the spade jack under the king, most normal declarers will assume your partner began with four spades, and will try to run that suit first for his discards (the right play if your partner is 4-4-3-2). This of course allows your partner to ruff in, and if he does not play a diamond now, you can always find another partner!

Sometimes third hand has the opportunity to follow with an honour to distract declarer from a winning route. The underlying concept is that, if declarer has a trump suit in which he might take a safety play – say:

A843

K1052

you can discourage him as East (with QJ96) by dropping an honour in a side suit at trick one to simulate shortage. Then declarer is unlikely to risk the safety play – as, if West gets in with the doubleton queen or jack, declarer may lose out to a ruff as well.

You can go one step further than this: it is hard to beat the following manoeuvre for bare-faced cheek. The defence was found by Liza Shaw, a British International, at the Rubber Bridge table.

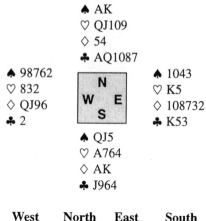

<pre>
                    ♠ AK
                    ♡ QJ109
                    ◇ 54
                    ♣ AQ1087
   ♠ 98762   ♠ 1043
   ♡ 832   N   ♡ K5
   ◇ QJ96   W   E   ◇ 108732
   ♣ 2   S   ♣ K53
                    ♠ QJ5
                    ♡ A764
                    ◇ AK
                    ♣ J964
</pre>

West	North	East	South
–	–	Pass	1NT
Pass	2♣	Pass	2♡
Pass	4NT	Pass	5♡
Pass	6♡	All Pass	

West led the club two, which declarer correctly assumed to be a singleton. He therefore went up with the ace, and Liza deposited the king underneath it! Naturally declarer now believed it was East who had the singleton club, and so he played the ace of hearts and a second heart, to avoid the risk of East getting a ruff from the doubleton trump. You can see the denouement of course. Liza won her heart king and gave her partner a club ruff.

Somewhere in the text-books is the classic deception in the trump suit, in defence to a slam, of a holding like this:

A104

J3 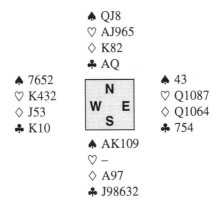 Q92

K8765

West led his long suit (in which East had a singleton) and declarer won in hand to lead a trump to the ace. When East dropped the queen under it, declarer knew enough to cross to hand for the safety play of leading up to the ten. Unluckily for him, West could win the jack, and give his partner a ruff. *Se non vero e ben trovato.*

The 1975 Bermuda Bowl was won by a narrow margin by Italy over the USA. This hand was more than their margin of victory. The Americans had played a sensible small slam – but the Italians had a major bidding accident to finish up in a terrible, but makeable Grand Slam of seven clubs.

♠ QJ8
♡ AJ965
◊ K82
♣ AQ

♠ 7652   ♠ 43
♡ K432   ♡ Q1087
◊ J53   ◊ Q1064
♣ K10   ♣ 754

♠ AK109
♡ –
◊ A97
♣ J98632

The West player had been confident that his club king would be a trick; he led a heart and declarer ruffed and played a club to the queen, then the club ace, finding the miraculous lie of the cards. But, if West had contributed the club king at trick two, declarer would probably take this at face value and he has a chance to make the contract if he believes this card is a singleton. If he simply were to draw trumps he would imagine he would have to lose a club trick – but he might succeed if East had four clubs and at least three spades.

He cashes the ace of hearts, three rounds of spades, two top diamonds and ruffs two more hearts. In this three card ending with the spade nine and the club jack-nine in hand, and the club queen and a heart and diamond in dummy, he ruffs his spade with the club queen and makes his last two trumps by a *coup en passant*.

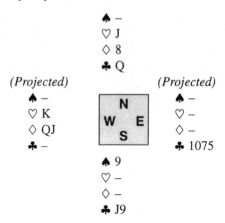

As the cards lie, this line fails when East can ruff the third spade. Would the great Giorgio Belladonna have fallen for this deception? Almost certainly, yes – his comment after the event was that, if West had played the club king, America would have been champions.

Sometimes bridge themes are like Number 12 Buses: you don't see a them for a long time – and then two examples come on consecutive days, as happened in the 1989 European Championships. This was the first:

Teams.

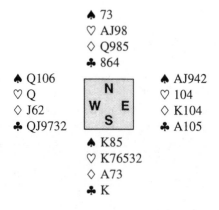

West	North	East	South
–	–	–	1♡
Pass	2♡	2♠	3◇
Pass	4♡	All Pass	

The defence led the club queen (thus potentially avoiding a disaster in that suit), and East took his ace and exited with a second club. Declarer ruffed, played a heart to the ace, then a spade towards his king. East took his ace and played another club; declarer ruffed, led the spade king and ruffed a spade, and drew the last trump. This was the five card ending:

Teams.

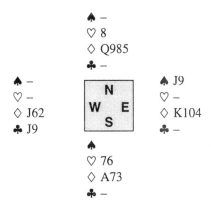

```
              ♠ –
              ♡ 8
              ◇ Q985
              ♣ –
  ♠ –                      ♠ J9
  ♡ –          N           ♡ –
  ◇ J62    W     E         ◇ K104
  ♣ J9         S           ♣ –
              ♠
              ♡ 76
              ◇ A73
              ♣ –
```

At this point declarer, who knew East to hold the diamond king from the auction, was well on his way to success; his intention was to lead the diamond three to the eight, to endplay East to lead a second diamond or give him a ruff and discard. However Nafiz Zorlu of Turkey in the West seat found the spectacular play of the diamond jack on this trick. Now declarer had to read whether this was the play of an unsupported honour, or from the jack-ten. In one case ducking the trick endplays West, in the other case the correct play is the queen from dummy. Perhaps justice was done when declarer ducked, allowing Zorlu to exit with a diamond for down one.

Holding Up on a Losing Finesse

Let us go one step further than one of the themes from the previous section. If we can see some point in not winning a trick with the cheapest card possible, why win the trick at all?

As usual, there are some technical reasons for the hold-up as well as the deceptive aspect. Let us just look briefly at a couple of layouts where you may have reason to hold up. (Note the emphasis; if dummy has no side entries these hold-ups may be pointless or even costly. They are most effective when dummy has exactly one entry outside the suit.)

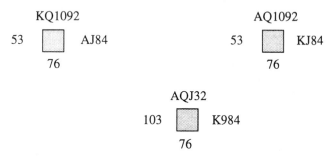

KQ1092
53   AJ84
76

AQ1092
53   KJ84
76

AQJ32
103   K984
76

East does not jeopardise his two tricks by ducking the first round of the suit, in any of our examples, but he does lose a tempo. Make up your mind whether dummy has 2+ entries, or no entries, in which case the duck costs a tempo, and maybe even a trick. If dummy has one entry, the duck will probably be right. And, for the purists, note that if declarer needs three tricks only from the third example and has one side-suit entry to dummy, he can duck the first round of the suit entirely as a safety play.

Having got the technical justification out of the way, let us look at why we might duck tricks. The most common reason is that we want to exhaust declarer's entries to dummy, or vice versa.

Some of these plays will become so automatic to you that you will not think of them necessarily as deceptive, but that is part of the story.

AQJ105
962   K87
43

AQJ10
965   K872
43

In both cases you can see that if dummy is entryless, then East saves at least one trick by ducking his king once. But wait a second; if it is right to duck with those North-South lay-outs, maybe it is worth investing a trick as East by ducking with a less rock-solid holding. Try these for size:

AQJ105

9762   K8

43

AQJ10

965   K87

432

In the first case we duck even though that would allow declarer to drop our honour on the next round, because we believe he is more likely to repeat the finesse. In the second case, we can duck twice, assuming declarer has enough entries to hand to take three finesses. Again, bear in mind that these plays are most effective if dummy has no side entries, or if you can see that declarer will waste valuable entries to hand repeating these finesses.

The following hand comes from the Spingold tournament in the US, and features one of the USA's top players. The play concerned looks unnatural – but so long as you have given the matter enough thought in advance, it should be logical enough.

Teams.

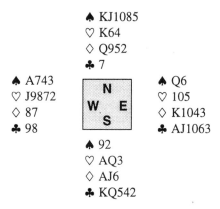

♠ KJ1085
♡ K64
◇ Q952
♣ 7

♠ A743
♡ J9872
◇ 87
♣ 98

♠ Q6
♡ 105
◇ K1043
♣ AJ1063

♠ 92
♡ AQ3
◇ AJ6
♣ KQ542

South played in 3NT, North having shown his spade suit on the way. West led a heart, which declarer took with the ace. When South ran the spade nine, Berkowitz in the East seat ducked – not an obvious play but, in theory and in practice, the winning move.

Why? Well, declarer surely has two or three small spades, and will repeat the finesse to your queen. If he has two spades you may (as in the real hand above) be able to cut him off from the spades altogether.

This is indeed what happened. Declarer naturally repeated the spade finesse and Berkowitz won the queen and returned a heart. Declarer finished up taking four tricks in the minors, three hearts, but only one spade trick, for one down.

(Note that it would also be the right play on this hand to duck in the East seat with Ax of spades (as opposed to Qx). In this instance it is more an entry destroying play than deception, but the results could be equally successful.)

The logic behind holding up with distributions including the ace is in part to exhaust declarer when he has a doubleton. In both these two following cases you also do best to duck the first trick so long dummy has no more than one entry.

KJ1092

875   AQ4

63

KJ982

Q75   A104

63

In the first case, you should duck when declarer leads to the nine if dummy has one entry, otherwise take the trick (with the ace or queen depending on the rest of the hand.) In the second case you should duck if declarer plays to the jack whatever the entry position (errors and omissions excepting).

The hand that follows incorporates a number of these themes, and in my opinion represents one of the great defences in bridge history – because it is a sequence of fine plays to beat a contract which, most of the time, would probably succeed with overtricks.

Teams.

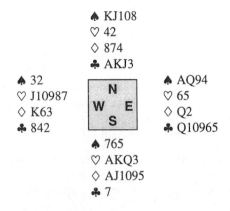

♠ KJ108
♡ 42
◇ 874
♣ AKJ3

♠ 32
♡ J10987
◇ K63
♣ 842

♠ AQ94
♡ 65
◇ Q2
♣ Q10965

♠ 765
♡ AKQ3
◇ AJ1095
♣ 7

After North had bid both the black suits South jumped to 3NT, and West naturally led the heart jack. Declarer immediately played a spade to the jack – and with this section being all about deception you are doubtless trying to work out why East (a great player and journalist, Herman Filarski) should duck this trick. In fact that would be a very poor play; Filarski won and returned a heart, to destroy declarer's entries to hand. Declarer won the second heart, played a spade to the ten, and East ducked.

Declarer happily played a diamond on which Filarski played the queen (an entry disrupting play) and South took this to play a third spade, allowing Herman to cash two spade winners. This is the ending:

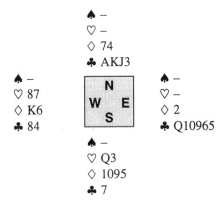

```
            ♠ –
            ♡ –
            ◇ 74
            ♣ AKJ3
♠ –                      ♠ –
♡ 87      ┌───────┐      ♡ –
◇ K6      │   N   │      ◇ 2
♣ 84      │ W   E │      ♣ Q10965
          │   S   │
          └───────┘
            ♠ –
            ♡ Q3
            ◇ 1095
            ♣ 7
```

When Filarski led a diamond West kept up the good work by ducking, and now declarer cashed his last top heart, dummy throwing a diamond and East a club. Declarer now knew the defensive shape, so he cunningly played the club seven to the ace (on which East unblocked the ten), and the club three from dummy. But Filarski allowed his partner to win the eight and cash two winners for two down. North innocently enquired whether it would have been better to run the seven of clubs from hand in the four card ending – but Filarski had his answer ready – he would have ducked it.

The following examples show another common distribution, which you could easily encounter every session. As usual, South is declarer.

```
        KQ102                          1086
J53     ┌─────┐    A94      A74     ┌─────┐     J53
        └─────┘                     └─────┘
         875                          KQ92
```

These distributions are to all intents and purposes identical, but it is a lot easier to duck the ace in the first example than in the second, where the honours are concealed. Of course, the point is that, if you win the ace at once, it is easy for declarer to finesse for the jack on the second round. If you duck the ace, declarer has to read the position very well.

Sometimes you have to steel yourself to a duck that appears highly unnatural; such as the following holdings.

```
        Q5                              Q5
1092  [     ]  K763          102  [     ]  K863
       AJ84                         AJ974
```

When declarer starts both suits by leading to the queen you have to duck in the first instance, in which case declarer will probably play your partner for Kxx, by ducking completely on the next trick, and subsequently laying down the ace. In the second example, declarer may finesse the nine on the way back if he has been convinced by a smooth duck from you.

Sometimes you need to duck an ace to preserve your entry to your own long suit. This example comes from the London Trophy, a contest designed primarily for non-experts. Occasionally a few ringers slip in – in fact as the event is designed for clubs, Friendly, Tennis or Golf, there is no reason for a team not to be full of reasonable players. This hand graced the Final of the event at the end of the Eighties – it would not have been out of place in a much more prestigious setting.

Aggregate Teams.

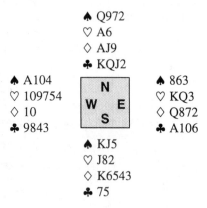

```
                    ♠ Q972
                    ♡ A6
                    ◇ AJ9
                    ♣ KQJ2
    ♠ A104          N          ♠ 863
    ♡ 109754    W       E      ♡ KQ3
    ◇ 10            S          ◇ Q872
    ♣ 9843                     ♣ A106
                    ♠ KJ5
                    ♡ J82
                    ◇ K6543
                    ♣ 75
```

Mike Hill was occupying the West seat on lead against 3NT (at the other table this contract had made comfortably from the North seat) and he made a good choice to lead the heart ten, not a small one, clearing up any ambiguity in the suit. His partner won the queen to return a small heart to the ace. Declarer rather forlornly played a spade to the king, and Hill ducked in perfect tempo – I was sitting behind him and I can vouch for it!

At this point declarer had to decide whether his Left Hand Opponent had the spade ace and not the club ace – in which case he should play on clubs now – or whether Hill had defended so well. I have a lot of sympathy with him for getting it wrong and playing a club. Now the defence could untangle their winners and beat the contract by two tricks. But, if West wins the first spade, the hearts are blocked and all declarer has to do is guess the diamonds to make his contract – and he will probably get a count on the hand to succeed in doing that.

Now, try this one for size! It won East the award for the best defence of the year in 1992, and he deserved it too.

Teams.

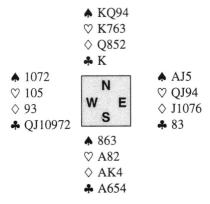

Imagine playing 3NT as South after a strong no trump and Stayman. You win the club lead and play a diamond to hand to try a spade to dummy's queen.

If East wins the ace and clears the clubs, you will test the diamonds, and eventually establish a spade trick without letting West get the lead. If East ducks, you may cross back to hand in diamonds to play a spade to the king, but if you win the next club you can still build a long spade without letting West get the lead. What happened at the table?

Declarer won the club lead, crossed to hand in diamonds and led a spade to the queen, on which East, Mike Passell contributed the jack! Declarer assumed that East had jack-ten or ace-jack-ten, and he crossed to hand to play a spade to dummy's king. Passell won the ace and played a second club, and West now had the entry of the spade ten to cash out his clubs.

A quite different reason for holding up on a losing finesse comes when declarer's strategy depends on whether the finesse wins or loses. If it wins, he can perhaps afford a safety play in trumps for instance. If that is the case, then we can get some mileage out of a discreet duck.

Teams.

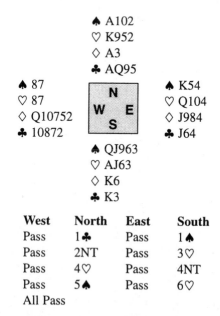

```
                    ♠ A102
                    ♡ K952
                    ◇ A3
                    ♣ AQ95
   ♠ 87                          ♠ K54
   ♡ 87          N               ♡ Q104
   ◇ Q10752    W   E             ◇ J984
   ♣ 10872        S              ♣ J64
                    ♠ QJ963
                    ♡ AJ63
                    ◇ K6
                    ♣ K3
```

West	North	East	South
Pass	1♣	Pass	1♠
Pass	2NT	Pass	3♡
Pass	4♡	Pass	4NT
Pass	5♠	Pass	6♡
All Pass			

On the lead of the diamond five South takes some time to win the king, and then takes the spade finesse. It is not too hard to work out that the only reason for taking the dangerous spade finesse before touching trumps is that South needs to know whether the spade finesse is working to judge how to play trumps.

Don't show him the spade loser; if you duck, South may think that he can afford the safety play in trumps of cashing the ace, and then leading low to the nine. Even if he has a trump loser, he 'knows' there is no spade loser. Not tonight Josephine.

It is arguable that this final distribution falls more appropriately in the section of giving declarer a losing option rather than ducking an ace; whichever category you want to put it into, it is a useful one to have seen in print – you need to be able to defend in tempo to get the most out of it.

Q4

J10   ☐   A75

K98632

Whether this is the trump suit or a suit at no trumps, declarer will presumably tackle it by leading to the queen. If you win the trick, declarer has only one distribution to play for to hold his losers to one – namely the jack-ten doubleton. Duck the trick, and declarer will probably play West for ace-ten doubleton.

Preventing the Blockage

We have already seen a couple of examples where we were on lead and trying to persuade declarer not to block our suit. There are also a couple of positions where we have to know how to follow so as to persuade our opponent to untangle our suits for us. In this section tempo is also especially important. We must make these plays without betraying the fact that anything unusual is going on.

97

A106542   ☐   KJ

Q83

You are East, defending 3NT after your partner has opened a weak two in this suit, and you know he has no side entry outside this suit. If this is the case, when partner leads a small card, try the jack at trick one – it will be almost impossible for declarer to duck this.

Two slight modifications on this.

J3   J3

A106542 ☐ K9   A96542 ☐ K10

Q87   Q87

In both these two cases you stand no chance of unscrambling your suit if you play the king on the first trick, but if you follow with your intermediate card declarer will almost certainly misread the position. Obviously you need to be confident that partner has no side entry to start attempting these plays – otherwise in some instances you may be throwing a trick or a tempo away. As I said earlier on, it is also important to make these plays in tempo – otherwise you risk tipping off both declarer and your partner to the position. The point is that, while declarer (at his own risk) can take any advantage he likes from your hesitations, your partner doubtless will (and should) bend over backwards to avoid drawing any inferences from irregularities in your tempo. So if you reveal that you have an honour by a break before playing your card, he may feel obliged to defend on the basis that you do not.

It does not have to be the doubleton king that is potentially jamming the works: this next example is a fine play by Michel Lebel, playing with Michel Perron of France, from the 1989 European Championships.

K5

A109843   Q3

J76

Lebel was sitting East and his partner (who had shown a six-card suit with a weak hand in the auction) led the ten, promising a higher honour. Declarer ducked in dummy, and so did Lebel! One can hardly blame declarer for failing to read the position and playing the jack.

Virtually the same East-West holdings:

J5

A109764   K3

Q82

Duck the opening lead of the ten and you give South a headache.

Preventing Declarer from Ducking

Yet again it helps to know the basic rules of technique before exploring the elements of deception. First of all let us look at when we should duck – and what we should do to overcome declarer's wiles.

On all the following five holdings you are sitting East, defending a no trump contract at teams, and your partner is leading your suit. You have only one sure entry outside this suit in the first four examples and no entry in case five, but you need to set up your suit to beat the contract.

(i)

```
        743
82    [    ]    KQ1095
        AJ6
```

(ii)

```
        QJ6
82    [    ]    K10975
        A43
```

In case (i) if you play the queen declarer can duck and kill the suit you must play the nine, and thus gain a tempo. In case (ii) it is an error for declarer to play dummy's queen or jack; if he ducks he neutralises the suit. But if he does err and you cover the jack (unless you have *two* entries, when covering is right) declarer can recover by ducking this trick.

(iii)

```
        AJ6
82    [    ]    K10975
        Q43
```

(iv)

```
        J64
82    [    ]    KQ985
        A103
```

(v)

```
        K43
82    [    ]    AQ1095
        J76
```

Think of yourself as Adam in the garden of Eden in example (iii), (iv) and (v). The snake in the form of a serpentine declarer may tempt you by playing dummy's jack or king respectively from dummy, but resist and play low, and you may reap a heavenly reward.

Those are the technical plays; now you need to focus on setting up your partner's suit, and overcoming declarer's possible ducking strategy.

```
                        A5
          108763       ☐       KJ2
                       Q94
```

Consider this suit in a no trump contract; your partner (whom you know from the bidding to have a very weak hand) leads the six. Declarer plays low from dummy, and if you make the natural play of the king you know that you will get exactly one trick from the suit. Try committing the heinous sin of finessing against partner, by playing the jack at trick one – now when declarer wins the queen (he will won't he?) you can clear the suit at your next turn by leading the king, and bingo! three winners. What if partner had the queen – then your play did not cost.

Of course this position arises in reverse when this is the layout:

```
                        A5
          1063        ☐       KJ872
                       Q94
```

When your partner leads your suit, and you have no quick entries, playing the jack preserves communication. But it helps to have your explanations ready for your partner if declarer has queen-nine doubleton.

More of the same:

```
                        95
          J8763       ☐       AQ2
                      K104
```

If your partner, having very limited values, leads the six, then it costs nothing to put in the queen at your first turn. After all if partner has the king there is no harm done, and if declarer has the king you effectively prevent him from ducking. But do remember that this play is only relevant when partner has a weak hand.

Let us see two similar hands to get the point properly. In both cases you are defending 3NT, after South opens a weak no trump.

Teams.

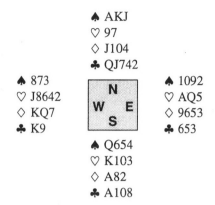

♠ AKJ
♥ 97
♦ J104
♣ QJ742

♠ 873
♥ J8642
♦ KQ7
♣ K9

♠ 1092
♥ AQ5
♦ 9653
♣ 653

♠ Q654
♥ K103
♦ A82
♣ A108

Teams.

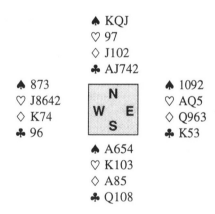

♠ KQJ
♥ 97
♦ J102
♣ AJ742

♠ 873
♥ J8642
♦ K74
♣ 96

♠ 1092
♥ AQ5
♦ Q963
♣ K53

♠ A654
♥ K103
♦ A85
♣ Q108

The first hand is a classic example of a little learning being a dangerous thing; if you play the heart queen at trick one, partner will win the club king and play you for the diamond ace rather than the heart ace.   In contrast, the second hand is exactly the right moment to play the heart queen – if you do not the defence will surely fail, but declarer has no chance if you play the queen in tempo. The critical point is that if you trance before making the play, a hot declarer will read the position – it would be a shame to waste your chance for glory, wouldn't it?

Teams.

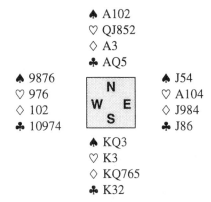

                    ♠ A102
                    ♡ QJ852
                    ◇ A3
                    ♣ AQ5

♠ 9876   ♠ J54
♡ 976   N   ♡ A104
◇ 102   W   E   ◇ J984
♣ 10974   S   ♣ J86

                    ♠ KQ3
                    ♡ K3
                    ◇ KQ765
                    ♣ K32

Look how easy the play in 6NT is, on the lead of the spade nine. Declarer knocks out the heart ace, and does not need even to test the diamonds when the major suit behaves.

But it is not that easy if East ducks the first two heart tricks. If hearts are 4-2 then declarer goes down at once by playing a third round. A much better percentage play is to test the diamonds first. All well and good if they behave – if not, go back to hearts, hoping that they are 3-3 and that the man with the ace had the short diamonds. Declarer is doubly unlucky, to run into this distribution and this defence.

Another way to look at the issue of not giving away information relates to the question of deceptive discards – we shall cover the topic under that category. At this point, however, it may suffice to say that the purpose of signalling and discarding is to give useful information to your partner.

If the only person who can benefit from a signal is declarer, there is no point in giving him a blue-print of your hand. Therefore, if you know that you who will have to take all the decisions, or you know that partner will not understand your delicate signal, then why bother to paint the picture?

In the European Championships played in Killarney in 1991, the winning British team generated a slam swing by very intelligent play at both tables.

Teams.

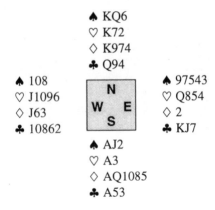

♠ KQ6
♡ K72
◇ K974
♣ Q94

♠ 108
♡ J1096
◇ J63
♣ 10862

♠ 97543
♡ Q854
◇ 2
♣ KJ7

♠ AJ2
♡ A3
◇ AQ1085
♣ A53

Both tables reached six diamonds from the South seat on the lead of the heart jack, and both declarers won the ace, drew trumps (East pitching two spades) and took the three top spades. Then they played a heart to the king and another heart. The Czech East (who did not want to get endplayed if he won the heart queen) ducked and the British declarer, Andy Robson, ruffed the trick, and correctly decided that East had the club king. So he played a club to the nine (yes, West should have played the ten) and endplayed East to give him a ruff and discard or play a club for him.

At the other table where John Armstrong was East, the defence took a slightly different turn; when the third heart was led Armstrong rose with the queen (pretending to be a man who *did* want to be left on lead). Declarer duly ruffed the trick, and was persuaded by this play that John did not have the club king. So he laid down the club ace, and went one down.

Trump Tricks

(Promotions, uppercuts, and general fooling around)

The opportunity to ruff, and over-ruff, is hedged around with deceptive elements. Sometimes you can achieve interesting results by over-ruffing high. Look at this trump suit – we have seen it before in a slightly different context).

Q872

4 ⬜ KJ63

A1095

West leads a card in a suit in which North and East are void. If East over-trumps dummy's eight with the jack that will be his last trick in the suit. But if he over-ruffs with the king he may score the jack later if South lays down the ace, preparing for a finesse against West's jack.

A slight variation on that theme:

J872

4 ⬜ Q1063

AK95

Whether East is over-ruffing dummy's eight, or following suit once West has switched to the four, he does best to play the queen. Either way declarer is likely to play West for the length.

Trump promotions and uppercuts are another tricky area. To understand them it is perhaps helpful to look at a few positions where the defence do best not to use their high trumps too soon.

When East leads a master card in a side suit in which West and North are void, West does best to discard rather than ruff in, when the trump suit is divided in the following ways.

92   92

Q5 ⬜ K73   J5 ⬜ K73

AJ10864   AQ10864

In either case if West scores his queen (or jack) that is the last trump trick for the defence; in the first case discarding assures the defence of two tricks, in the second case declarer has to guess the trumps to hold his losers to one. Note that in both cases, if East leads a losing plain card and South covers it, the defence does best to ruff in with the five, to force the over-ruff, leaving declarer an awkward guess on the next round. And of course that means it would probably be right as West to ruff low with king-five also.

Sometimes it is right not to over-ruff dummy in order to generate extra trump tricks, or to put declarer to the guess again. In the next two examples you are East, and declarer ruffs a card in dummy with a high trump in a suit in which you are also void.

When declarer ruffs with the queen you assure your side of three tricks by not over-ruffing in case one. In the second example your chances of two tricks are much better if you do not over-ruff, since declarer may lead his nine next.

Two more positions where the defence maximise their chances by not over-ruffing; in each case dummy has ruffed with the ten, and you, as East, increase your chances of getting three and two tricks respectively by not winning the trick.

In the first example declarer may take the finesse of the eight on the first or second round if you refrain from the over-ruff, and in the second case declarer may try and drop your partner's doubleton queen.

All sorts of strange things can happen if you refrain from taking your trump tricks at the first chance you get. Here you are defending four spades, and you lead a diamond in response to your partner's opening pre-empt.

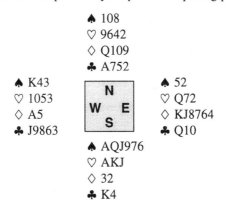

♠ 108
♡ 9642
◇ Q109
♣ A752

♠ K43
♡ 1053
◇ A5
♣ J9863

♠ 52
♡ Q72
◇ KJ8764
♣ Q10

♠ AQJ976
♡ AKJ
◇ 32
♣ K4

When declarer ruffs the third diamond high you do not over-ruff, and when declarer crosses to table to run the spade eight you duck that too. Now is declarer's last chance to take the heart finesse – but I don't think he will, do you?

Sometimes the decision not to over-ruff can look like a quixotic rejection of a trick; but it can come back in the most surprising ways.

Pairs.

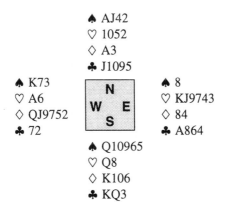

♠ AJ42
♡ 1052
◇ A3
♣ J1095

♠ K73
♡ A6
◇ QJ9752
♣ 72

♠ 8
♡ KJ9743
◇ 84
♣ A864

♠ Q10965
♡ Q8
◇ K106
♣ KQ3

West	North	East	South
–	–	2♡	2♠
3♡	3♠	All Pass	

North-South appear to have done well to stop so low; on the sight of dummy you can see that desperate measures may be called for. Your partner signals encouragement on your opening lead of the heart ace, so you play a second round, and on the third round declarer ruffs with the spade nine, and you discard the club seven.

Now if declarer swallows the bait, and plays a spade to the ace and a second spade, you win your king and play a club to your partner for a club ruff.

An even more unusual opportunity presented itself to a French expert pair from thirty years ago.

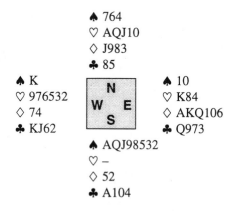

```
                    ♠ 764
                    ♡ AQJ10
                    ◇ J983
                    ♣ 85
      ♠ K                      ♠ 10
      ♡ 976532      N          ♡ K84
      ◇ 74        W   E        ◇ AKQ106
      ♣ KJ62        S          ♣ Q973
                    ♠ AQJ98532
                    ♡ –
                    ◇ 52
                    ♣ A104
```

Pierre Jais opened one diamond in third seat, but South brushed this aside by bidding four spades, and there the matter rested. On Dominique Pilon's lead of the diamond seven the defence played three rounds of the suit, and declarer ruffed with the jack. Pilon's decision not to over-ruff looks quixotic – but he could see that the trick should come back – and it did with interest!

Declarer naturally played the ace of clubs and a second club, allowing Jais to lead a fourth diamond. Declarer ruffed with the queen, and now Pilon had his trump trick back.

Sometimes your best chances of creating a trump trick is to appear to be creating one for your partner ....

North/South Game. Teams.

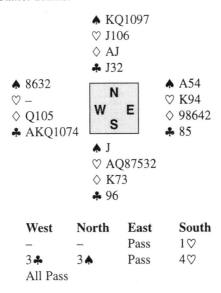

♠ KQ1097
♡ J106
◇ AJ
♣ J32

♠ 8632
♡ –
◇ Q105
♣ AKQ1074

♠ A54
♡ K94
◇ 98642
♣ 85

♠ J
♡ AQ87532
◇ K73
♣ 96

West	North	East	South
–	–	Pass	1♡
3♣	3♠	Pass	4♡
All Pass			

At this vulnerability West's three club bid, though technically intermediate, could be anything.

Your partner elects to lead three top clubs against four hearts (perhaps it would have been better to switch to a diamond in theory, although it would not work here) and on this trick you may find that ruffing with the heart nine (in an attempt to appear like a man desperately promoting a trump for your partner) is your best move. You may be able to persuade declarer to lay down the heart ace now – if you do not ruff South is likely to play you for the heart king.

This final hand is another example of manipulating trumps in an unusual fashion, again from a high standard American pairs event.

Let us consider it first of all as a declarer play problem, before seeing all four hands.

Game All. Pairs.

♠ Q
♡ AQJ64
◇ K8732
♣ K4

♠ J742
♡ 832
◇ A9
♣ 9832

West	North	East	South
–	–	Pass	Pass
1♠	2♠	Pass	3♡
All Pass			

North's cuebid showed a two suiter with hearts and a minor.

West leads a top spade and switches to the club jack. You play the king, but East cashes the ace and queen, then exits with the spade ten which you ruff in dummy. You cross to the diamond ace and take a successful heart finesse, then play the diamond king, on which West follows with the queen, and ruff a diamond with the three, overruffed with the king. West exits with the spade king, which you ruff high in dummy, as East follows to reach this ending:

♠ –
♡ A6
◇ 87
♣ –

♠ J
♡ 8
◇ –
♣ 98

It looks as if you have a complete count on the hand: West started life with a 5-2-2-4 shape, and you can ruff a diamond in hand, a club in dummy, and then take the heart ace and concede the last trick. So you confidently ruff a diamond to hand. Unlucky!

This was the full hand.

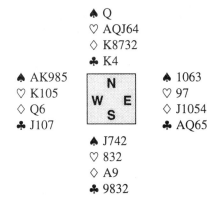

            ♠ Q
            ♡ AQJ64
            ◇ K8732
            ♣ K4

♠ AK985   ♠ 1063
♡ K105   ♡ 97
◇ Q6   ◇ J1054
♣ J107   ♣ AQ65

            ♠ J742
            ♡ 832
            ◇ A9
            ♣ 9832

When you ruff the diamond West over-ruffs, and plays another spade, promoting her partner's heart nine for the setting trick.

Kitty Munson's decision to over-ruff with the 'known' heart king made declarer's life impossible; if she had over-ruffed with her low trump, declarer would certainly have drawn a round of trumps in the four card ending, and given up a diamond for nine tricks.

4
DECEPTIVE DISCARDING

False Attitude

We have already seen in the section on card play how we can signal deceptively, and give false suit-preference when following suit. This principle can obviously be extended to discarding as well.

Game All. Teams.

```
                    ♠ K102
                    ♡ 103
                    ♢ K832
                    ♣ AJ95
      ♠ J954         ┌─────────┐      ♠ Q873
      ♡ Q2           │    N    │      ♡ A86
      ♢ J1075        │  W   E  │      ♢ A96
      ♣ Q82          │    S    │      ♣ 1063
                     └─────────┘
                    ♠ A6
                    ♡ KJ9754
                    ♢ Q4
                    ♣ K74
```

West	North	East	South
–	–	–	1♡
Pass	2♣	Pass	2♡
Pass	3♡	Pass	4♡
All Pass			

North-South had an unopposed auction to four hearts on a spade lead, and East passed the first test for the defence by putting in the spade seven at trick one. Declarer won his ace, led a spade to the king and led the heart ten to the queen. West played a spade to East's queen and declarer ruffed and knocked out the heart king, then ruffed the fourth round of spades, pitching a club from dummy. When he drew a third round of trumps, West took the opportunity to discard a low club. As South was marked with six tricks in the majors, and two minor suit cards, it was necessary to assume his minor suit honours were the diamond queen and the club king, or else there would be no defence. That being so, she needed to put declarer off the club finesse. The plan worked perfectly. Declarer now discarded a diamond from dummy, and played the diamond queen from hand, ducked, then a second diamond won by East, who exited with a third diamond. Declarer ruffed this trick, eventually reducing to this position with three clubs in either hand.

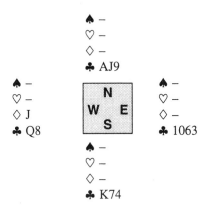

Having seen the early club discard from West, he tackled the suit by leading the ace and then the jack, trying to pin West's ten, which of course led to going two down.

Frequently the defence can work out relatively early on that declarer may be reduced to a guess with a king-jack. If you can diagnose the problem early enough you can help to push declarer in the wrong direction.

Let us say that the lay-out of the critical suit is along these lines:

105

Q986   ⬚   A742

KJ3

As West you know that unless declarer has the jack he cannot misguess the suit; so you should assume he does have that card, and discard the eight or nine at your first turn.

Sometimes things are more desperate than that.

```
        J5                            J5
Q1074  [  ]  A862        Q862  [  ]  A1074
        K93                           K93
```

In the first example you might persuade declarer to go wrong if as West you discard the ten, to create a finesse position for declarer. Similarly you might fool a gullible declarer in the second example as East if you pitch the ten – but he would have to be very gullible.

One of the general principles that applies to defence is that frequently one defender has enough of the outstanding high cards to be in control of the defence. So long as he gets accurate information from his partner he will know what is going on, and he does not have to discard honestly because his partner has nothing to contribute to the play. (Of course a thoughtful declarer can benefit from this if he can identify who has the residual values – but it is not as easy for him as the defenders.)

One of the ways that a declarer can solve guesses involving king-jack combinations and guesses involving the location of a queen is simply to look at whether a hand discards in the key suit, not the size of the card discarded. This principle follows a dictum first defined in print nearly 20 years ago by Terence Reese, which is still as valid today as it was then. The concept is that there are certain honours from which it is easier to discard than others.

To explain this further, let us take a simple example, and without following it through to a definite conclusion, just consider the general probability.

In a contract of four spades dummy has an unbid club suit of: 10532. West leads a trump and declarer draws three rounds of trumps. East throws a club on the third round. Is he most likely to have started with the ace, king, queen or jack?

Reese's comment was that defenders find it much easier in abstract to discard from length in suits where they have the ace or king, a good point. (Because they have a top card they are not worried about the discard setting up the suit.)

Therefore, in our example, East is more likely to have the ace or king, or indeed nothing, than to have discarded from three or four cards to the queen or jack.

What is the conclusion you can draw from this? Well, as a declarer playing against players up to a moderate standard, I would assume that their discards follow Reese's rule. As a defender, you need to be aware of the way that declarer's mind may work, and cross him up wherever possible. Let us look at an example in practice against a declarer whom we know to be capable of watching our cards.

Game All. Pairs.

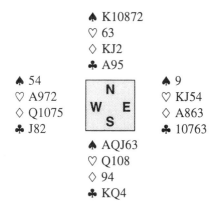

♠ K10872
♡ 63
◇ KJ2
♣ A95

♠ 54
♡ A972
◇ Q1075
♣ J82

♠ 9
♡ KJ54
◇ A863
♣ 10763

♠ AQJ63
♡ Q108
◇ 94
♣ KQ4

The opposition bid simply one spade – four spades, and your partner elects to lead a trump. Declarer plays two trumps immediately, on which you should consider avoiding the discard of a diamond; although it can almost never cost a trick in the suit, it may well help clear up a guess for declarer. For example, you would be reluctant to discard a diamond if you had Q863 in case declarer had, for example, A754 or, indeed, virtually any hand with four diamonds.

False Count

One of the most useful pieces of information that declarer can obtain from the discarding is that most defenders try to make their discards in safe suits as early as possible. They save their tricky discards for when they have found out more about the hand.

What that tends specifically to mean is that defenders frequently will discard in their own suits (because they know that declarer will not establish long cards in those suits) and, if there is no suit bid and supported by the defence, then the defenders will typically pitch from a five card suit, in preference to a four card suit or a three card suit.

Again an example may be helpful to sort out how declarer may profit from automatic discarding.

East/West Game. Teams.

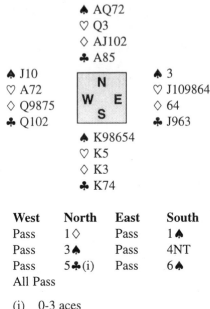

	♠ AQ72		
	♡ Q3		
	◊ AJ102		
	♣ A85		

♠ J10   ♠ 3
♡ A72   ♡ J109864
◊ Q9875   ◊ 64
♣ Q102   ♣ J963

♠ K98654
♡ K5
◊ K3
♣ K74

West	North	East	South
Pass	1◊	Pass	1♠
Pass	3♠	Pass	4NT
Pass	5♣(i)	Pass	6♠
All Pass			

(i)   0-3 aces

You lead the spade jack, for want of anything better to do, and declarer draws three rounds of trumps. Your partner throws the heart jack and a small heart; in your method that suggests an even number of hearts. What is your first discard?

Well, assuming that your partner's carding makes sense, he ought to have six hearts to the jack. You can afford a small diamond of course, but the risk is that you will tip declarer off to your length in the suit, and allow him to take the simple diamond finesse. Pitch a heart, rise with the ace of hearts and return the suit; at least you make declarer work harder for his contract.

Here is another example from Louis Watson's classic, 'The Play of the Cards' which in fact is given as a declarer play problem rather than a defensive conundrum. See what you make of it; you are in the West seat.

East/West Game. Teams.

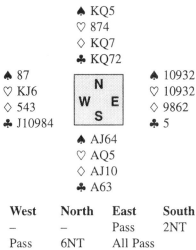

               ♠ KQ5
               ♡ 874
               ◇ KQ7
               ♣ KQ72

♠ 87   ♠ 10932
♡ KJ6   ♡ 10932
◇ 543   ◇ 9862
♣ J10984   ♣ 5

               ♠ AJ64
               ♡ AQ5
               ◇ AJ10
               ♣ A63

West	North	East	South
–	–	Pass	2NT
Pass	6NT	All Pass	

When you lead the club jack and see fifteen points in dummy it does not take a magician to realise partner has nothing, and that in abstract your chances of beating the contract are fairly slim. However you do have well placed heart honours, so all hope is not yet lost. Declarer wins the ace of clubs in hand and rattles off four rounds of spades. Make your discards.

To have any chance of beating the contract you must assume that partner has some decent heart intermediates. The point is that if you throw a club at any point declarer will cash all the side-suits to throw you in with the fourth round of clubs. So you must keep all your clubs, and the obvious conclusion is that you must bare your heart king to do that. (That is why partner needs good heart intermediates. If declarer sees the heart jack appear he will have his twelfth trick if he has the heart ten.)

Having decided to bare the heart king, you have to weigh up deception against other factors. The most deceptive moment to bare your heart king would be now; on the fourth spade you could throw your second heart. Declarer will test the clubs and find the 5-1 split, and might then lay down the heart ace, intending to cross to dummy and play a heart up to the queen if the king did not appear. My preference would be to throw one heart (maybe the jack) and a diamond on the spades, and then to pitch the low heart on the third round of diamonds if necessary. That is a reasonable combination of caution and deception. So long as you hold on to your clubs, at the very least you make declarer struggle for his living.

False Suit Preference

Deceptive suit preference is a delicate affair, in particular because it is an area where only the better declarers are going to be capable of watching and understanding the message you are sending your partner. In other words you may find yourself misleading your partner, and find that declarer is not watching your cards at all.

Having expressed that caveat, let us look at a hand where you might be able to fool declarer – depending on how carefully he is considering the significance of your cards.

North/South Game. Pairs.

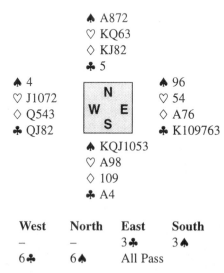

```
              ♠ A872
              ♡ KQ63
              ◇ KJ82
              ♣ 5
  ♠ 4                          ♠ 96
  ♡ J1072      N               ♡ 54
  ◇ Q543    W     E            ◇ A76
  ♣ QJ82       S               ♣ K109763
              ♠ KQJ1053
              ♡ A98
              ◇ 109
              ♣ A4
```

West	North	East	South
–	–	3♣	3♠
6♣	6♠	All Pass	

A fairly random auction by three out of the four players at the table (it is only pairs after all!) sees South in a surprisingly good contract. You lead the club queen to South's ace, and declarer draws two rounds of trumps with the king and ace. What should you discard?

I think the club two might be construed as suit preference for diamonds, and that seems a good idea. You know declarer is either going to make his contract, by playing you for the diamond queen if he is missing the heart ace, or the actual lay-out exists, in which case the hand is all about the diamond guess. The best you can do to mislead declarer is to show preference for diamonds. Next, if necessary, you may have to pitch a diamond to show you do not have the delicate holding of the sort you actually have.

Make Life Hard for Declarer

The principle here is one of not giving additional information to declarer by allowing him to count out your hand precisely or inferentially. The danger in discarding things you do not want is that when you show out of a suit, you make declarer's count of the hand much easier. Two examples follow where players who ought to have known better made slight slips, and were appropriately punished.

North/South Game. Pairs.

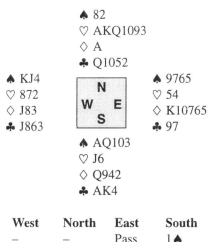

```
              ♠ 82
              ♡ AKQ1093
              ◇ A
              ♣ Q1052
  ♠ KJ4                      ♠ 9765
  ♡ 872          N           ♡ 54
  ◇ J83      W       E       ◇ K10765
  ♣ J863         S           ♣ 97
              ♠ AQ103
              ♡ J6
              ◇ Q942
              ♣ AK4
```

West	North	East	South
–	–	Pass	1♠
Pass	2♡	Pass	2NT
Pass	6NT	All Pass	

This hand is from the 1993 Epson International Simultaneous Pairs. South showed a strong no trump and North went for the highest scoring Matchpoint slam. West led a passive heart, and declarer cashed the ace and king of clubs, and ran the hearts as East threw a high-low in diamonds. What actually happened at the table was that West (a former World champion) threw three diamonds, and declarer played a spade to the queen and king.

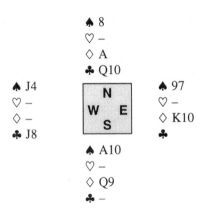

In the four card ending West returned a low club to the queen and East threw a spade, and South threw a diamond. Now the diamond ace forced a spade out of West, and declarer knew that both defenders only had one spade left, so he played a spade to his ace. Obviously declarer can always make the contract, but do you see the defensive error? West knew she was going to have to throw a spade, so she should have thrown one on the sixth heart. Then declarer does not get the complete count on the diamond suit, and has to guess the spade suit in the ending.

North/South Game. Teams.

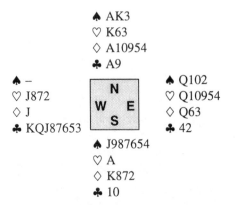

This board came from the 1994 Sunday Times Invitation event, and at almost every table West opened five clubs, and North doubled to show cards. South removed to five spades and North raised to six spades. Declarer on Vu-graph, Robert Sheehan of Great Britain, won the club lead, and in preparation for the 3-0 trump split, unblocked the heart ace, crossed to the spade ace, finding the bad news, and ruffed a club. Now a second trump to dummy, and the king of hearts and a heart ruff, allowed South to throw East in with the third trump. This was the ending:

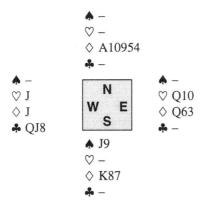

```
              ♠ –
              ♡ –
              ◇ A10954
              ♣ –
  ♠ –          N          ♠ –
  ♡ J       W     E       ♡ Q10
  ◇ J          S          ◇ Q63
  ♣ QJ8                   ♣ –
              ♠ J9
              ♡ –
              ◇ K87
              ♣ –
```

Stripping off the side-suits may not have seemed to accomplish much, but East now chose to exit with a heart. When declarer ruffed he now saw West follow to the heart, and therefore had an inferential count that West had an 8-4-1-0 shape. Accordingly Sheehan played a diamond to the ace and took a finesse on the way back to make his contract. Again East was slightly at fault in clearing up the residual ambiguity in the count of the hearts. If he had exited with the diamond six (he knows declarer is 7-4-1-1 and thus his only chance is to find his partner with the diamond jack) declarer still has a real guess in the ending.

Defending Against Squeezes

Defending against the squeeze is one of the most difficult parts of the game. We are not talking about breaking up the squeeze, to prevent it from operating; that is clearly a matter of technique for the most part, rather than deception. Rather we want to focus on what happens when the squeeze appears to be inevitable.

Let us look at the most trivial sort of way to defend against a squeeze that is just about to bite us.

North/South Game. Pairs.

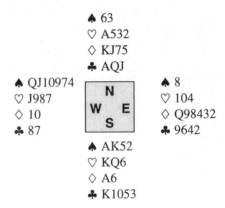

```
              ♠ 63
              ♡ A532
              ◇ KJ75
              ♣ AQJ
♠ QJ10974                   ♠ 8
♡ J987          N           ♡ 104
◇ 10        W       E       ◇ Q98432
♣ 87            S           ♣ 9642
              ♠ AK52
              ♡ KQ6
              ◇ A6
              ♣ K1053
```

Because of the vulnerability you open three spades (you do not have to like it) and North doubles for take-out, allowing South to jump to 6NT.

On the lead of the spade queen declarer ducks, and then wins the next spade. Now declarer cashes the diamond ace and king, then four rounds of clubs to reach this ending.

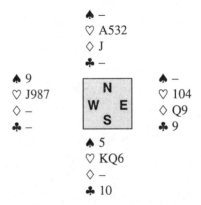

```
              ♠ –
              ♡ A532
              ◇ J
              ♣ –
♠ 9                         ♠ –
♡ J987          N           ♡ 104
◇ –         W       E       ◇ Q9
♣ –             S           ♣ 9
              ♠ 5
              ♡ KQ6
              ◇ –
              ♣ 10
```

It is always correct tactics to pitch your spade, and leave it up to declarer to cudgel his brains to recall if the spade five is now high. He should get it right – but it is easier on paper than in real life, where lapses of concentration are not infrequent.

That was a bit trivial – let us look at some more testing areas. Frequently you become aware that you will have to bare an honour some time before the crucial moment comes along. Don't wait until the crucial moment and then agonise over the decision. Make the critical discard as early as you can, and try to avoid unnecessary breaks in tempo.

Of course if your opponents respect you that may not be enough ....

North/South Game. Teams.

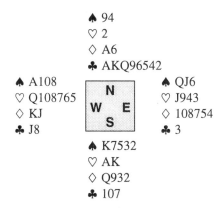

♠ 94
♡ 2
◇ A6
♣ AKQ96542

♠ A108
♡ Q108765
◇ KJ
♣ J8

♠ QJ6
♡ J943
◇ 108754
♣ 3

♠ K7532
♡ AK
◇ Q932
♣ 107

On this hand from the European Championships of 1991 Hans Vergoed of Holland was in the West seat, defending against six clubs, after South had opened one spade and he had overcalled two hearts. He might have made a rather speculative double to avoid the heart lead, which as it happens would have saved himself a lot of bother, but he didn't, and his partner led a heart.

Declarer thoughtfully cashed both of dummy's hearts before running eight clubs and Vergoed could see that he was going to be squeezed in a three card ending.

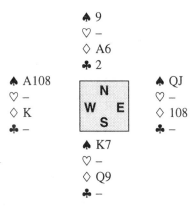

♠ 9
♡ –
◇ A6
♣ 2

♠ A108
♡ –
◇ K
♣ –

♠ QJ
♡ –
◇ 108
♣ –

♠ K7
♡ –
◇ Q9
♣ –

Declarer knew that West had the high cards, so when East threw a spade he threw dummy's spade seven. Vergoed had seen that he was going to be squeezed, and had carefully bared his diamond king early, so that he could pitch a spade at this point, hoping that North would think he still had two diamonds left and would try to throw him in with a spade. Unfortunately North had too much respect for him, and correctly assumed that he would bare his diamond king rather than be endplayed – so he cashed the diamond ace now; a painful if flattering compliment.

This deal from the Bermuda Bowl in 1989 has a very similar theme. Again two experts met, and a game of bluff and double bluff ensued.

Teams.

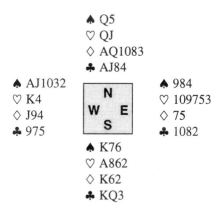

```
                 ♠ Q5
                 ♡ QJ
                 ◇ AQ1083
                 ♣ AJ84
  ♠ AJ1032      ┌─────────┐      ♠ 984
  ♡ K4          │    N    │      ♡ 109753
  ◇ J94         │ W     E │      ◇ 75
  ♣ 975         │    S    │      ♣ 1082
                └─────────┘
                 ♠ K76
                 ♡ A862
                 ◇ K62
                 ♣ KQ3
```

Patrick Huang of Taiwan reached the slightly aggressive slam of six no trumps, and won the club lead in hand. He played a spade to the queen, then ran all his minor suit winners, on the first of which Mari of France discarded the heart four. As he could tell, declarer was able to reduce to a three card ending, and on the last diamond Mari threw the spade jack – trying to look like a man with the bare spade ace left.

Alas for his plans, Huang decided that that was exactly how a World Champion would defend, and played a heart to his ace.

This is a rather different approach to a not dissimilar theme; you are West defending against six clubs on an old fashioned Acol auction, on a hand where you have a pretty good idea that partner's values are limited.

Teams.

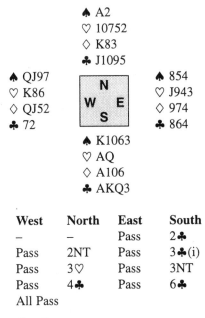

♠ A2
♡ 10752
◇ K83
♣ J1095

♠ QJ97
♡ K86
◇ QJ52
♣ 72

♠ 854
♡ J943
◇ 974
♣ 864

♠ K1063
♡ AQ
◇ A106
♣ AKQ3

West	North	East	South
–	–	Pass	2♣
Pass	2NT	Pass	3♣(i)
Pass	3♡	Pass	3NT
Pass	4♣	Pass	6♣
All Pass			

(i)   Baron

You lead the spade queen, and declarer plays three rounds of the suit, ruffing in dummy, crosses to hand with the club queen and ruffs a fourth spade as your partner throws a diamond. Now declarer plays off three more round of clubs; you discard …?

Beware; if you throw a diamond declarer will play off three rounds of the suit, endplaying you to lead into his heart tenace at trick twelve. To have a chance to defeat the contract you should pitch two hearts, baring your heart king to keep four diamonds. If declarer starts to strip off the diamonds, remember to follow with an honour on the second round as if you started life with QJ5. Then when declarer throws you in with the diamond ten you can cash the two of diamonds at trick twelve.

Squeeze Me, Please

One of the most enjoyable achievements at the bridge table is to fool declarer into believing that he has squeezed you so that he opts for a losing line rather than a straight finesse, which any pedestrian toiler could take. Two points to bear in mind here; first of all it is fairly pointless to try to achieve this against anyone but a competent and thoughtful player, who will actually watch your cards and pick up the message you are trying to send. Secondly the rules of bridge require you to limit your simulated distress to the cards you play. Writhing in anguish when you have no problem is unfortunately not permitted – although there are many games of bridge which seen closer to the 'All-in' style, where anything goes.

Sometimes you can convey your fake message by your suit preference, and the order of your cards; here we are just looking at an overtrick, but it is Match-point pairs.

Game All. Pairs.

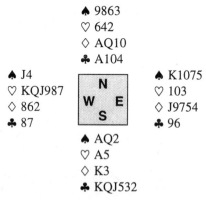

```
                    ♠ 9863
                    ♡ 642
                    ◇ AQ10
                    ♣ A104
    ♠ J4                          ♠ K1075
    ♡ KQJ987        N             ♡ 103
    ◇ 862         W   E           ◇ J9754
    ♣ 87            S             ♣ 96
                    ♠ AQ2
                    ♡ A5
                    ◇ K3
                    ♣ KQJ532
```

This is a difficult six clubs slam to bid; after South opens one club you jump to two hearts pre-emptively; North makes a take-out double, and South jumps to three no trumps. You lead the heart king, to partner's ten, and declarer's five. At this point you can see the contract is safe, but cutting down on overtricks may be vital. You continue with the heart queen, implicitly a suit preference signal for spades. When declarer runs six rounds of clubs you start by throwing the heart jack; then declarer cashes three rounds of diamonds. On the last one you throw the spade jack, reducing to the spade four and heart nine. With any luck declarer will believe he has squeezed you and play to drop the spade king rather than take the finesse.

If you can see no genuine chance of beating the contract, one tactic which is guaranteed to start declarer's mind racing is the under-ruff.

Game All. Pairs.

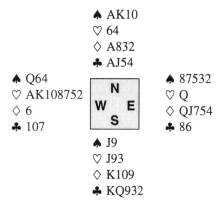

West opens three hearts, doubled by North for takeout, and South bids five clubs. It is hard to see an alternative to the spade finesse, but watch what happens on the defence of three rounds of hearts, if East under-ruffs at trick three.

South, believing that East has a good reason for preserving his side suit cards, runs all his trumps, reducing to this position.

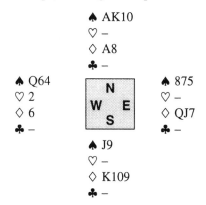

On the last trump East lets go of a spade, and declarer cashes two top diamonds. On the basis of what has been discarded so far, declarer is quite likely to play to drop the spade queen rather than finesse.

An even more unusual under-ruff, with an underlying technical theme to it, won its perpetrator the 1989 Defence of the Year award.

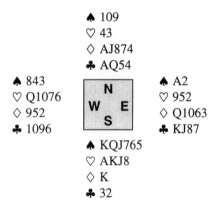

It is rarely correct to lead a trump against a small slam, but on this particular occasion declarer would be hard pressed to make even eleven tricks on a spade lead. However, West led a diamond against six spades, and declarer won the king, cashed two hearts and ruffed a heart, then took dummy's two aces. He ruffed a club back to hand, and ruffed his last heart in dummy, in this ending.

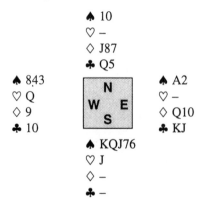

You can see that East can not achieve anything by an over-ruff in this position, and it is also apparent on a second glance that, if he discards a club, declarer ruffs that suit back to hand, and exits with a top spade, and the defence can still accomplish nothing. Similarly, if East pitches a diamond, declarer ruffs a diamond, and when East is in with the spade ace he no longer has a diamond to play to promote his partner's eight of spades.

However our hero, Dung Duong of Switzerland, resourcefully under-ruffed, and now declarer had a real problem. He chose to ruff a club to hand and play the spade king. Duong won his bare ace and exited with his last club, to promote a trump trick for his partner.

Beautifully done, however, one might argue that this was more a case of superb technique than deception. But to do that would be to overlook the fact that declarer had a chance to make the contract by playing East to have found this fine play, and exiting at the critical moment with a low spade to drop East's singleton ace. Of course if South is capable of doing this, then next time East would have started life with eight-two of spades, not ace-two, when the under-ruff is again the only chance to trouble declarer.

Magnus Lindqvist of Sweden found a variant on this theme from the European Championships in 1979.

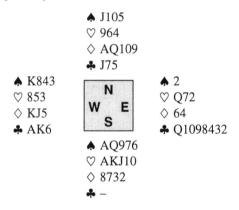

                    ♠ J105
                    ♡ 964
                    ◇ AQ109
                    ♣ J75
    ♠ K843   ┌─────────┐   ♠ 2
    ♡ 853   │   N   │   ♡ Q72
    ◇ KJ5   │ W   E │   ◇ 64
    ♣ AK6   │   S   │   ♣ Q1098432
                    └─────────┘
                    ♠ AQ976
                    ♡ AKJ10
                    ◇ 8732
                    ♣ –

Lindqvist as West led a top club against four spades, and declarer ruffed, crossed to the diamond queen, and ran the spade ten, ducked, then played a spade to the queen and ace. Lindqvist led two more rounds of clubs, on which declarer discarded diamonds to retain trump control.

In this ending:

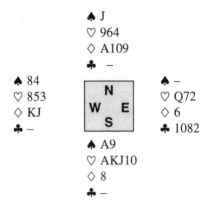

♠ J
♡ 964
◇ A109
♣ —

♠ 84   ♠ —
♡ 853   ♡ Q72
◇ KJ   ◇ 6
♣ —   ♣ 1082

♠ A9
♡ AKJ10
◇ 8
♣ —

West led another club on which declarer threw a heart, and Lindqvist ruffed, instead of discarding a heart! Declarer was convinced that West had the heart queen, and thus he could be squeezed. So he over-ruffed in dummy, crossed to his ace of hearts and cashed his two trumps, on which Lindqvist finally let go of a heart. Now declarer crossed to the diamond ace, and played to drop the heart queen rather than taking the finesse, for one down.

Of course, if declarer can squeeze you, you must legally be entitled to repay the compliment. On the following hand from the European Junior championships of 1988, Spyros Liarakos of Greece had to do at least two good things before he could turn the screw. (Of course this is not technically a play involving your discards, since in practice it is a problem for declarer, but this seems the most appropriate section for an amusing hand.)

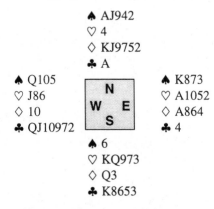

♠ AJ942
♡ 4
◇ KJ9752
♣ A

♠ Q105   ♠ K873
♡ J86   ♡ A1052
◇ 10   ◇ A864
♣ QJ10972   ♣ 4

♠ 6
♡ KQ973
◇ Q3
♣ K8653